T0311481

The Wellbeing of Children under Three

Now in an updated second edition, *The Wellbeing of Children under Three* unravels what wellbeing means for this age group by making clear links between research and effective early years practice. It looks at what wellbeing means for under threes in the light of key aspects of international social policy, and practically demonstrates how practitioners can support children in this area.

Focusing on the home-setting partnership with parents, work attitudes, adult–child interaction and quality learning environments, the book explores the role that adults play in holistically supporting children's individual personal, social and emotional needs. This new edition also includes new material on practitioner mental health and the Leuven scales as a measure of wellbeing. Each chapter features:

* clear explanation of relevant theories
* case studies and examples of good practice
* focus points for readers
* questions for reflective practice

Providing a wealth of practical ideas and activities, this handy text encourages the exploration of all aspects of babies' and toddlers' wellbeing to help practitioners ensure effective outcomes for the youngest children in their care, and is essential reading for all those working with the under threes.

Helen Bradford is an independent Early Years Consultant, based in Cambridgeshire. She has worked in the early years sector for over twenty years and has published extensively during this time.

Supporting Children from Birth to Three
Series Editor: Sandy Green

The most rapid and significant phase of development occurs in the first three years of a child's life. The *Supporting Children from Birth to Three* series focuses on the care and support of the youngest children. Each book takes a key aspect of working with this age group and gives clear and detailed explanations of relevant theories together with practical examples to show how such theories translate into good working practice.

Each title in this series includes the following features:

- clear explanation of relevant theories
- case studies and examples of good practice
- focus points for readers
- questions for reflective practice

Collectively, the series provides practical ideas and activities to help practitioners develop appropriate indoor and outdoor environments, appreciate the importance of the planning cycle and gain a better understanding of all aspects of babies' and infants' wellbeing.

Titles in this series include:

Appropriate Environments for Children under Three
Helen Bradford

Planning and Observation of Children under Three
Helen Bradford

The Wellbeing of Children under Three, 2nd Edition
Helen Bradford

For more information about this series, please visit: www.routledge.com/Supporting-Children-from-Birth-to-Three/book-series/SUPPCHILDREN

The Wellbeing of Children under Three

Second Edition

Helen Bradford

Routledge
Taylor & Francis Group

LONDON AND NEW YORK

Second edition published 2021
by Routledge
2 Park Square, Milton Park, Abingdon, Oxon OX14 4RN

and by Routledge
52 Vanderbilt Avenue, New York, NY 10017

Routledge is an imprint of the Taylor & Francis Group, an informa business

© 2021 Helen Bradford

First edition published by Routledge 2012

British Library Cataloguing-in-Publication Data
A catalogue record for this book is available from the British Library

Library of Congress Cataloging-in-Publication Data
A catalog record has been requested for this book

ISBN: 978-0-367-53013-6 (hbk)
ISBN: 978-0-367-53014-3 (pbk)
ISBN: 978-1-003-08010-7 (ebk)

Typeset in Optima
by Newgen Publishing UK

Contents

Illustrations

Tables

Figures

Plates

Introduction

The Wellbeing of Children under Three is one of a series of three books providing relevant, supportive and accessible material for those working with the very youngest children, from birth to three years old. The premise for all three books is twofold: all babies and young children are (a) social beings and (b) competent learners – but, importantly, from birth. The other two titles in the series are *Appropriate Environments for Children under Three* and *Planning and Observation of Children under Three*.

The books are designed for all early years professionals and adults working with babies and children under three in their early years settings who are seeking ideas on how to optimise best practice using the resources they have available to them. The books explore theories and principles behind good practice in each of the title areas outlined, and include case studies, examples and focus points for readers, as well as suggestions for staff development. The books are written for the early years practitioner, a specialist perceived as someone who is in a privileged position to work with this age group; someone who is able to see and respond to each child they encounter as the unique person that they are.

A key question for the book is how can every child's wellbeing be ensured as they evolve and grow to make sense of the world around them? *The Wellbeing of Children under Three* relies on a staff team that can work collaboratively to develop ways of providing high-quality learning environments, so that all the children in the team's care feel full of wellbeing in that they are secure, happy and able to thrive. Feeling secure and happy and being able to thrive means, paradoxically, that children must also feel able to take risks appropriate to their stages of development: to explore, enquire and experiment as their knowledge and understanding of the environments they inhabit grow. Children develop language and communication skills, which enable them to communicate in and navigate those environments and experiences. They develop the physical and creative skills necessary to experience the exciting and intriguing spaces that unfold before them. They begin a journey of understanding that will support and equip them for their life ahead. The key message of this book, therefore, is that a child's wellbeing is paramount if projected expectations surrounding physical and personal, social and emotional development are to take place; in other words, wellbeing is central to children 'doing well'.

The book takes a reflective, child-led approach where good practice begins with honest evaluation and ongoing, transparent discourse among practitioners. All chapters build on each other, while containing the same core messages. Chapter 1 outlines a working definition of wellbeing in relation to children under three; problematic in itself owing to the rather unstable nature of the term. It does allow for several lines of thinking to be explored within the overall book, however. Chapter 2 explores children's personal, social and emotional wellbeing in some depth, creating strong links with theory and considering whether it is possible to measure wellbeing. Chapter 3 looks at personal wellbeing – that of the practitioner. It also looks at wellbeing within the early years setting as a whole, and the impact of staff wellbeing on the care environment. Chapter 4 investigates aspects of adult interaction with children under three, focusing in particular on effective communication skills to support wellbeing. Chapter 5 discusses the issues and considerations behind developing high-quality environments to support children's wellbeing, with Chapter 6 offering a conclusion and drawing together the main threads of the key messages presented. Coverage within the book is wide, ranging from wellbeing, rest and sleep, to wellbeing and inclusion.

This second edition of *The Wellbeing of Children under Three* is again dedicated to my niece Jenii and her family.

Wellbeing matters

 ## An introduction

Increased awareness in children's wellbeing from an early age includes different categories for consideration. The World Health Organization (WHO), for example, defines wellbeing as a state of complete physical, mental and social wellbeing; not merely the absence of disease or infirmity (WHO, 1948). Early intervention during childhood has been shown to have long-term benefits in terms of overall resilience and ability to manage in later life (Taggart *et al.*, 2015). To this end, wellbeing supports the notion of 'good' citizenship and our future ability to contribute usefully to society. In England, the National Institute for Health and Care Excellence (NICE, 2012) separates wellbeing into three different categories: emotional, psychological and social. In addition, NICE identifies a wide range of factors that ought to be considered. These aspects range from factors such as happiness and confidence and having good relationships with others, to managing emotions and an individual's capacity for resilience.

Activity: a working definition

Before proceeding further with this chapter, develop a working definition of child wellbeing within your early years setting. Include statements related to children's physical, mental and social wellbeing. Do this as a staff group if you are working through the chapter together.

Now consider the following section on wellbeing and children's rights.

Wellbeing and children's rights

At first glance, the phrase 'children's rights' might not automatically be the first thought that comes to mind when thinking about the under-three age group; however, interest in children's rights has become an increasingly prevalent concept worldwide since 1959 with the Declaration of Rights of the Child by the General Assembly of the United Nations. The Declaration acknowledges children as being those aged from birth to 18 years. Thirty years later, in 1989, world leaders officially recognised the rights of the child by signing the UN Convention on the Rights of the Child, a 54-article document which states that every child has the same rights. These rights appear under five umbrella headings, outlined below:

1. The right to a childhood. Childhood is recognised as a crucial time for growth and development, but also as a time of potential vulnerability, which means that children need extra protection compared to adults.

2. The right to be educated. Articles relating to education include specific references to children who are disabled.

3. The right to be healthy. Every child has the right to health care, clean water, nutritious food and a safe environment so they can be as healthy as possible (Article 24).

4. The right to be treated fairly. All children have the same rights, no matter where they are from, what their family background may be or whether they are disabled or not. Currently in the UK, the fifth richest country in the world, around four million children live in poverty.

5. The right to be heard. Article 12, for example, states that all children have a right to be able to give their opinion when adults are making a decision that will affect them, and adults should take that opinion seriously.

In addition, there are several Articles that deserve attention when thinking about the subject matter of this book, in that wellbeing should be of paramount importance for early years settings when considering the children in their care. The Articles are listed below with links to early years principles of care, children's learning and their development:

- Article 3. All organisations concerned with children should work towards what is best for each child. Working towards what is best for each child should be the primary aim of every early years setting, fundamentally reflected through their mission statement, their aims and their ethos, as well as their practical provision and pedagogy within the care environment. The phrase 'working towards' suggests a reflective approach, one that allows for response, evaluation and change where appropriate. It also suggests a collaborative approach among members of staff who collectively represent 'the organisation' or the setting, and who together develop appropriate environments, learning and developmental opportunities for every child based on individual need.

- Article 16. All children have the right to privacy. Sometimes children simply need to be quiet. They need a space in which they can be undisturbed. A quiet area in the setting will allow for such privacy when children wish to withdraw for whatever reason, whether to sleep, read a book or play alone. Babies need privacy and concentrated one-to-one attention during intimate moments such as nappy changes. Changing a nappy while carrying on a conversation with another member of staff, talking over the child or ignoring them sends out poor signals to them and is a sign that their privacy during this intimate time is not of the practitioner's uppermost consideration. Degotardi and Davis (2008) asked early years practitioners to comment on videotaped extracts of their interactions with a child in their care during a nappy-changing routine. While not always the case, many of the practitioners gave descriptive responses that contained more information about the practitioner's behaviour than that of the child, with some responses not referring to the child at all:

> I'm changing [child's] nappy at the moment. I put the paper down. I'm taking her nappy off. Pull out the tub – put it in the bin. I'm talking to her – make sure she's ok. Give her a wipe. Throw the wipe away. Put on a new nappy – pants back on then we're up. Then that's it.
>
> (Degotardi and Davis, 2008: 229)

This may be a scenario perhaps to reflect on in relation to current setting baby room practice.

- Article 30. Children who come from a minority group have the right to learn and use the language and customs of their own families. Inclusive practice should be a prime concern for all early years settings, in that it should reflect some aspects of babies' and children under three's homes, communities and cultures: for example, using images and messages that represent home experiences and that recognise cultural diversity. Practitioners should work towards an understanding and respectful acknowledgement of a child's culture, because this may have an impact on appropriateness in relation to provision of care.

- Article 31. All children have the right to relax and play, and to join a wide range of activities. This article is exemplified within the high number of early years curricula supporting principles of learning through play. Further, children under three need to experience a learning and care environment that offers many opportunities for exploration and enquiry and that enables them to further their understanding of the world around them as they grow and develop.

Activity: staff discussions

1. How is Article 31, which states that all children have the right to relax and play and to join a wide range of activities, exemplified within your setting?

2. Go back to each of the five umbrella headings from the UN Convention on the Rights of the Child. What evidence can you provide to show how you support each of these elements within your setting's approach to *childcare*? Make notes under each heading to return to later in the chapter.

At the heart of the UN Convention on the Rights of the Child is a concern for every child's wellbeing – wellbeing in relation to an acceptable standard of living; quality of family life; coordinated care; health; food; sleep; being safe; and having equal opportunities. The list could go on, but the equation is simple: when all of the above are satisfied, a child's wellbeing is respected, responded to and replete. They will then have the foundational means with which and in which to thrive. The precepts of the Convention are particularly pertinent for early years practitioners, because they sit well within current research suggesting that it is the quality of early life experiences, including interactions with others, that later impacts on life outcomes for children (Taggart *et al.*, 2015). Such research findings are further acknowledged and addressed within the new pre-emptory Early Years Foundation Stage (EYFS) for children in England aged between birth and five years old (DfE, 2017). This is a document committed to ensuring that effective support is available for every child so that they are enabled to achieve later success, both in the realm of education, and also for life itself. While it can be argued that 'success' is a rather subjective term to use in itself (it begs the question by which or whose definition, for example), the ultimate aim of the EYFS (DfE, 2017) is to support every child's wellbeing with a clear focus on personal, social and emotional development, communication and language skills, and physical skills as the backbone or foundation to ensure successful future outcomes. These foci corroborate the WHO's inclusion of physical, mental and social wellbeing within its definition of what is meant by wellbeing.

Supporting children's wellbeing within the early years setting

Activity: staff discussions

Part 1
- How are children's rights recognised within your setting?
- What opportunities are in place to promote children's interests?
- How do you know that children feel safe in the setting?
- What procedures are in place to ensure that all children, whatever their age, can voice their opinions and be heard?

Perhaps each staff member could be encouraged to present a case study of one of the children in their care, responding specifically to the above four questions. Or if your setting works in age-related rooms, or teams, case studies could be presented a year group at a time for whole-staff discussion.

> ### Part 2
>
> - Does a review of practice in relation to supporting children's rights need to be undertaken within the setting? If so, who will take responsibility for leading such a review?
> - How could such a review feed into a setting policy on children's wellbeing?

Wellbeing and young children

Education is one area in which the concept of wellbeing features strongly within documentation and where it is constructed as both instrumental in, and an outcome of, personal development (Ereaut and Whiting, 2008; Sylva *et al.*, 2010). It has been established within this chapter, however, that it is difficult to think about wellbeing as a single construct in relation to very young children. Pollard and Lee's seminal literature review from 2003 suggests five distinct domains of child wellbeing: physical, psychological, cognitive, social and economic. These are listed below, with examples of suggested links to babies and children under three for the early years practitioner to consider:

1. Physical. The physical domain is concerned with a child's physical health, their rate of growth, their knowledge about eating healthily and staying safe. It is important, for example, for the early years practitioner to have a strong working knowledge and understanding of child development in order to be able to respond to a child's developmental needs, but also to be able to raise any concerns early on, for example, if a child is not walking within the projected timescale. While ultimately a concern may not become an issue for intervention (my own son did not walk until he was a good 18 months old and although concerns were raised, in the end no intervention was required), to raise it is the right professional response. Doing so means that you as the practitioner are no longer trying to manage on your own; you can plan accordingly, as well as having support from other professionals who may need to be involved.

2. Psychological. The psychological domain encompasses mental health, anxiety levels and psychosocial aspects such as self-esteem, confidence and emotion. Alexander (2010: 164) argues for 'the importance

of good mental health in order to sustain mutually satisfying personal relationships'. In literature related to early childhood, the term 'emotional wellbeing' is synonymous with Pollard and Lee's (2003) psychological domain. Bird and Gerlach, for example, argue that emotional health and wellbeing is 'the subjective capacity and state of mind that supports us to feel good about how we are and confident to deal with present and future circumstances. It is influenced by our emotional development and how resilient and resourceful we feel ourselves to be' (2005, cited in Roberts, 2006: 6). Children and self-esteem will be returned to and looked at in some detail in Chapter 2.

3. Cognitive. The cognitive domain is concerned with healthy brain development from birth onwards, and subsequently across the lifespan. Cognitive development for babies and children under three is akin to Jean Piaget's sensorimotor stage; the first stage of a child's life. During this period, children learn about the world by using their senses to interact with their surroundings. They therefore benefit from stimulating surroundings and interactions. Cognitive development is crucial for understanding and producing language. At the setting, it is crucial to support a child's communication skills and their language development; knowing how to do this is a particular skill for the early years practitioner to feel secure in.

4. Social. The social domain encompasses sociological perspectives such as family and peer relationships, communication skills and the availability of emotional and practical support. One of the elements of good practice with children under three is strong communication between the home and the setting. Developing strong relationships with a family is essential in order to develop appropriate care plans for individual children, because understanding family relationships will affect provision. The early years practitioner must also know how to be emotionally available for the children in their care: for example, understanding why a child is crying and what the cry is telling them. Is it a tired cry? A hungry cry? A cry in response to being hurt in some way? Knowing how to respond appropriately is a crucial element of early years care.

5. Economic. The economic domain involves family income and wealth, economic hardship and availability of and access to economic support such as government benefit systems. While it is important not to automatically make assumptions about single-parent families, for example, or children from certain socio-economic backgrounds, awareness on the part of the early years practitioner is important.

The idea of domains is a useful one when considering the wellbeing of babies and children under three because it enables a holistic approach. Consider the following in relation to one child at one particular moment in time:

- A family support officer may be more concerned with the economic aspects of the child's wellbeing.

- A health visitor may have the physical aspects of the child's wellbeing foremost in their mind.

- The early years practitioner may have social and cognitive aspects of the child's wellbeing as their primary concern.

While it is important not to lose sight of the global, or holistic, nature of wellbeing, it is also important not to assume that a positive or negative assessment in one domain necessarily means that the child's wellbeing as a whole corresponds to this assessment. It is also important that those people involved in the child's overall wellbeing work together to ensure that appropriate support is in place.

Activity

Compare the five umbrella headings of the UN Convention on the Rights of the Child with Pollard and Lee's (2003) five domains. Save your notes to refer to later in the chapter.

For reflection in the setting

1. Return to the notes that you have been making throughout this chapter. How does your setting currently support the holistic nature of wellbeing, as outlined above, for every child?

2. Create a list as a staff team.

3. How do you know that everyone involved with each child is working together 'to ensure that appropriate support is in place'? Can improvements be made? If so, identify those improvements and develop an action plan to address any gaps in provision.

Case studies: mapping Pollard and Lee's (2003) five domains of wellbeing to early years approaches and curricula

1. New Zealand's Te Whāriki

Te Whāriki is underpinned by a vision for children who are competent and confident learners and communicators, healthy in mind, body and spirit, secure in their sense of belonging and in the knowledge that they make a valued contribution to society. Wellbeing is one of five strands that feed into an environment of learning and development for children aged between birth and five years; the other four are belonging, contribution, communication and exploration. Table 1.1 outlines the strand of wellbeing. Note the progression within the strand that leads to children being able to take ultimately greater control and agency for themselves.

Within the strand of wellbeing, very young children experience an environment where their health is promoted, their emotional wellbeing is nurtured and they are kept safe from harm. Wellbeing as described here maps well to Pollard and Lee's physical and psychological domains; however, other domains are incorporated within other strands. Pollard and Lee's social domain, for example, comes under Te Whāriki's second and fourth strands, belonging and communication.

Table 1.1 Wellbeing within the Te Whāriki

STRAND	GOALS	LEARNING OUTCOMES
Wellbeing	Children experience an environment where:	Over time and with guidance and encouragement, children become increasingly capable of:
	their health is promoted	keeping themselves healthy and caring for themselves
	their emotional wellbeing is nurtured	managing themselves and expressing their feelings and needs
	they are kept safe from harm	keeping themselves and others safe from harm

Source: www.education.govt.nz/early-childhood/teaching-and-learning/te-whariki/

- Belonging: Children *and their families* experience an environment where connecting links with the family and wider world are affirmed and extended; they know that they have a place, they feel comfortable with the routines, customs and regular events, and they know the limits and boundaries of acceptable behaviour.

- Communication: Children experience an environment where they develop non-verbal and verbal communication skills for a range of purposes; they experience the stories and symbols of their own and other cultures, and they discover and develop different ways to be creative and expressive.

Te Whāriki's third and fifth strands, those of contribution and exploration, align with Pollard and Lee's cognitive domain:

- Contribution: Children experience an environment where there are equitable opportunities for learning, irrespective of gender, ability, age, ethnicity or background; they are affirmed as individuals and they are encouraged to learn with and alongside others.

- Exploration: Children experience an environment where their play is valued as meaningful learning and the importance of spontaneous play is recognised; they gain confidence in and control of their bodies, they learn strategies for active exploration, thinking and reasoning, and they develop their theories for making sense of the natural, social, physical and material worlds.

There is an argument to suggest that contribution would also feed into Pollard and Lee's economic domain in terms of giving children future life chances.

It is interesting that while links can be made, Te Whāriki's strand of wellbeing does not in itself map consistently to the five domains. Ereaut and Whiting argue that 'wellbeing is a cultural construct and represents a shifting set of meanings – wellbeing is no less than what a group or groups of people collectively agree makes "a good life"' (2008: 1). Following this line of thinking, because it is such a challenge to define wellbeing per se, it is important to consider how the setting in which we work considers the term. Being clear will lead to stronger, coordinated outcomes for children.

2. Economic wellbeing and the English early years context: the 'Funded Twos' initiative

In England, expanding pre-school provision for two-year-olds has been a specific focus since 2012 as part of a government initiative of early education entitlement for this age group (DfE, 2013). On the one hand, it would follow that two-year-olds are perceived by the government as a prioritised age group with unique educational needs. It has been established within the realm of neuroscience, for example, that the emergence of communication and language skills happens during a particular window of brain development for children; thus, children's experiences from birth to three years old are critical in relation to longer-term outcomes as certain fundamental skills are subject to time-specific development. Much more is now known about the benefits of nutrition and physical exercise as components of neurological growth and development. This knowledge has impacted the structure of the EYFS in England (DfE, 2017), with its three prime areas for child development.

On the other hand, it could be argued that such an initiative of early education entitlement serves to highlight a particular social construction of the child (Moss, 2010). The pre-school provision the initiative describes is primarily intended for a group of children covered by the term 'Funded Twos'. They are the recipients of a targeted government policy intervention aimed at 'lower income families' for whom the local authority has a statutory charge to identify to take up a free early education place (DfE, 2013: 2). As Moss (2010) argues, our view of the child is socially constructed within particular contexts, which then underpin policy approaches. It therefore follows that the current Funded Twos approach begins with a deficit pedagogical model in line, for example, with Malaguzzi's (1993) understanding of the 'poor' cultural child; the child for whom it is assumed additional support will, by default, be required. As Funded Twos places can be determined by family income alone, this policy approach ascribes an assumptive deficit perspective in relation to socio-economic status.

Activity

Return to your original definition of wellbeing. Is there anything you could now adjust or amend to develop it? Try to make your definition personal to your setting and the children in your care. In this respect:

1. It might be helpful to revisit your mission statement or defined ethos. Where can you find the notion of wellbeing within your policy documentation?
2. Return to the notes you made for the Activities in this chapter. Where can you find the notion of wellbeing within your responses?

Save the definition to return to at a later time.

For reflection in the setting

- Could you map the early years curriculum that you follow within your setting to Pollard and Lee's five domains?
- How do you make sure that you do not make assumptions about particular children in your care, as in the example of the Funded Twos?

Maslow's Hierarchy of Needs

Maslow's Hierarchy of Needs offers a scaffold framework of human need that develops over five levels, from basic to higher-level needs. Maslow first introduced his Hierarchy of Needs in his 1943 paper, 'A theory of human motivation'. The hierarchy suggests that individuals are motivated to fulfil basic needs before moving on to other needs; indeed, Maslow's theory suggests that the most basic level of needs *must* be met before the individual will strongly desire (or be able to focus motivation upon) those higher-level needs. There are five different levels in Maslow's Hierarchy, each outlined briefly here in ascending order, reflected upon with babies and children under three in mind:

1. Physiological needs. Physiological needs include the most basic needs that are vital to survival, such as the need for water, air, food and sleep. Maslow believed that these needs are the most basic and instinctive needs in the hierarchy, because all needs become secondary until these physiological needs are met. One of our first responses to a baby who is crying might be to check whether they are hungry or not. An upset two-year-old may also be hungry, or in need of sleep.

2. Security needs. This set of needs is about babies and children under three feeling safe and secure within their environment, including being happy to be left in the setting once their parents or carers leave.

3. Social needs. Social needs include needs for belonging, love and affection. Relationships with families and early caregivers help to fulfil this need for babies and children under three where the child feels loved, valued and accepted. A setting that adopts a key person approach may indeed be supporting Maslow's notion of social need. A key person accepts overall responsibility for a child or children within the setting, becoming a familiar person who the child accepts and responds to. The key person provides continuity of care for an individual child and acts as a key link between home and the setting, ensuring that close communication with parents is maintained. It is through this relationship that understanding of an individual child's needs and appropriate responses can be maintained.

4. Esteem needs. After the first three needs have been satisfied, esteem needs become increasingly important. These include the need for things that reflect on self-esteem, personal worth, social recognition and accomplishment. A key person can play a vital role in relation to esteem needs within the setting; they are the specialist who understands and responds to individual young children's needs, both physical and emotional. The key person is the person who knows the child well and is aware of all the special details of how they are cared for, helping them to feel cherished and able to express themselves fully, to relax and to feel confident that they matter. The key person becomes the child's safe, secure and consistent base to return to, physically and emotionally.

5. Self-actualising needs. Self-actualisation needs are the highest level of Maslow's Hierarchy. Once the four other levels of need have been fulfilled, the young child is able to fulfil their potential. This is when babies

and children under three are essentially in the optimum position to thrive. As a result of child wellbeing, healthy development and learning can take place.

Maslow's Hierarchy of Needs is often portrayed in the shape of a pyramid, with the largest and most fundamental levels of needs at the bottom, and the need for self-actualisation at the top (Figure 1.1).

Maslow's Hierarchy begins at the bottom with a consideration of the child's physical requirements; these are perhaps basic (but nonetheless vital) needs to ensure survival, such as having enough of the right kind of food to eat and water, juice or milk to drink. The fulfilment of physical needs allows a child to be comfortable; they do not feel hungry or thirsty. They have had enough sleep and rest. The next set of needs involve the need for a child to feel safe within the environment: at home, in the setting and also in the wider community.

The middle of the pyramid addresses the emotional fulfilment of the young child, who must feel loved and have a sense of belonging in order to feel comfortable within their surroundings. It is one thing to join a group of children, but the child must feel accepted and recognised to feel truly welcome within the setting. Children need to be introduced to each other, for example, no matter how young they are. They need to spend time in each other's company. The early years practitioner should use each child's name so that other children pick up and learn what other children in the setting are called. When reading a book with two children, for example, encourage each to take turns turning the pages. Scaffold the experience by saying 'It's Isla's

Figure 1.1 Maslow's Hierarchy of Needs

turn to turn the page . . .'; 'Now it's Joseph's turn to turn the page'. Support children by using their names: 'No Isla, it's Joseph's turn now. Let Joseph turn the page. It's your turn next!' Making children feel welcome by displaying their photographs in a prominent place within the setting is another way of supporting those who attend, as if this is their space.

Discussion

How else could you support a developing sense of ownership among children within your setting? Think about each age group in turn: birth to one year; one to two years; two to three years.

Let us look at Maslow's Hierarchy another way, at what each hierarchical element means in relation to the early years environment:

- Self-actualisation: where the environment (including those who participate in it and what is offered in terms of provision) provides stimulation, challenge and opportunities to use children's talents.

- Self-esteem: where the environment (including those who participate in it and what is offered in terms of provision) makes children feel individually valued.

- Love, affection and belonging: where the environment (including those who participate in it and what is offered in terms of provision) promotes ownership and belonging and social interaction; makes children feel known and cared about as individuals.

- Safety needs: where the environment (including those who participate in it and what is offered in terms of provision) makes children feel safe and secure.

- Physiological or survival needs: where the environment (including those who participate in it and what is offered in terms of provision) meets children's physical needs.

Maslow's Hierarchy of Needs suggests exactly what the children in our care need in terms of immediate and future self-actualisation. A strong foundation must be built in order for the other levels to build one upon the other. Each level must be strong in order to get to the next level, and so on. If one level is weak for a child, this will have an impact on the quality of achievement of subsequent levels, because all five interrelate.

A goal of every early years setting caring for babies and children under three should be to accommodate every level of the pyramid. Whether through group activity, circle time or individual attention, each and every child should receive the best attention and experience possible, in order to fulfil every need and achieve optimum progression. Maslow's Hierarchy of Needs supports a clear explanation of child wellbeing: of how wellbeing can be supported through the individual needs of very young children being attended to and fulfilled in order for them to feel comfortable within their environment, but also, importantly, to feel comfortable within themselves. Children need to learn about and understand who they are; once they become accustomed to their surroundings and their peers, they then need opportunities to develop their knowledge through purposeful and age-appropriate learning experiences. In this way, optimum learning can occur, and children's wellbeing is protected.

Activity

1. Map Maslow's Hierarchy of Needs to your previous mapping of the five umbrella headings from the UN Convention on the Rights of the Child and Pollard and Lee's five domains of wellbeing. What similarities are apparent? Are there any differences?

2. From the information you now have in front of you, how can you ensure that the children within your setting are being cared for and supported to thrive within the frameworks outlined in this chapter?

3. Revisit your definition of wellbeing created at the beginning of this chapter. Do you need to add to or rephrase your original response?

4. Develop a case study of one of the children in your care. Perhaps you are their key person. How is self-actualisation realised for this child in the setting? Outline how each level of need is fully supported according to Maslow's Hierarchy.

Chapter conclusion

If a goal for early years practitioners working with babies and children under three is to keep track of each child's individual wellbeing, then each setting will need to have a clearly defined concept of the term. This chapter has explored a holistic overview of child wellbeing, interrogating its meaning, beginning with the UN Convention on the Rights of the Child and then drawing on Pollard and Lee's (2003) physical, psychological, cognitive, social and economic domains of wellbeing. Another framework, Maslow's Hierarchy of Needs, has been introduced. The chapter has encouraged early years practitioners to consider the notion of wellbeing within their setting by taking a reflective and considered approach.

 # Resources for further exploration

Maslow, A.H. (1943) A theory of human motivation. *Psychological Review*, 50 (4): 370–396.

Pollard, E.L. and Lee, P.D. (2003) Child well-being: a systematic review of the literature. *Social Indicators Research*, 61: 59–78.

Te Whāriki: www.education.govt.nz/early-childhood/teaching-and-learning/te-whariki/

The UN Convention on the Rights of the Child: www.unicef.org.uk/what-we-do/un-convention-child-rights/

The World Health Organization and early child development: www.who.int/topics/early-child-development/en/

Personal, social and emotional wellbeing

Measuring personal, social and emotional wellbeing within the early years setting

While it might be argued that babies and children under three cannot express their subjective preferences to measure their wellbeing, researchers such as Mayr and Ulich (2009: 45) argue that the wellbeing of children under a practitioner's care 'is of paramount importance beyond all pedagogical methods and trends'. Children learn best when they are both healthy and happy. It therefore follows that the wellbeing of very young children could be used as a key indicator of the quality of provision within an early years setting. While empirical research in children's wellbeing may be scarce, observation scales have been developed to look at elements of 'how children are' in their early years settings. Three examples are outlined below, looking at babies and children under three in the relative immediacy of the moment, and, importantly, looking at their approach to a situation they might find themselves in, as opposed to trying to assess their learning outcomes.

Bowlby's Attachment Theory

Children must feel secure in their learning environment if they are going to be able to learn and develop within it. Laevers (1996) discusses the importance of children's emotional stability for learning and development; people with a high level of confidence and self-esteem are more likely to be content and effective in their lives. All this points to the need for babies and children under three to have access to, and to belong within, a learning environment that is warm, secure and positive, and where they can feel happy, healthy, safe and comfortable: descriptive adjectives that support and echo the precepts of wellbeing outlined and explored within Chapter 1 of this book.

The premise for this book is twofold: all babies and young children are (a) social beings and (b) competent learners from birth. Research has shown that during the first year of life, babies are in the active process of forming social relationships and emotional ties (or attachment) with their primary caregivers (Wallach and Caulfield, 1998; David, 2009). Between seven to nine months of age, babies begin to show unmistakable signs of attachment, such as crying to signal distress and clinging to maintain physical closeness when they are separated from their caregivers.

Three major theorists offer insight into the notion of attachment: Sigmund Freud, Konrad Lorenz and John Bowlby. Briefly, Freud argued that early interactions between children and caregivers determine eventual personality and social development. Lorenz believed that attachment evolved during the course of human evolution because it promotes a young child's survival. In more detail, Bowlby (1969) believed that the earliest bonds formed by babies with their caregivers have a tremendous impact that continues throughout life. In his view, because of a baby's relative helplessness at birth, built-in mechanisms maintain their proximity to their caregivers in order to ensure their protection. Known as Attachment Theory, Bowlby argued that one of the most important bonds a baby can make is with the primary caregiver, a relationship sometimes referred to as the infant–mother attachment relationship, as it is typically the mother who fulfils such a role in the baby's early life. Not all babies experience the same quality of early interactions with their mothers, however. To achieve positive outcomes, young children are said to need unconditional acceptance from the significant people in their lives, although studies have shown that individual differences in infant–mother attachment security can be attributed to variation in maternal sensitivity (Braungart-Rieker et al., 2001). Mothers of 'secure' babies have been observed to be more reliable, consistent, sensitive and accepting of their children than mothers of insecurely attached babies. In social interactions where a baby's behaviour succeeds in eliciting a positive and sensitive response from the parent, they will feel encouraged to continue the behaviour (Parker-Rees, 2007). However, babies and young children are also able to recognise mismatches between what they hear and a person's body language, and such incongruities can confuse them.

Bowlby's Attachment Theory is used here to offer a framework for understanding young children's emotional needs and to explain and predict emotional development. To this end, understanding and responding appropriately to young children's emotional needs is a key factor in promoting their wellbeing. Children's emotional needs include feeling a sense of security and belonging and having a sense of self-esteem. Emotional needs must be met in order to support a child's developing maturity, independence and autonomy; their ability to learn with confidence, to develop social skills, friendships and rewarding relationships; and their ability to regulate their emotional responses and to respond to the emotional needs of others. In addition, neuroscience confirms the importance of emotional engagement in learning. Advances in neuroscience and the development of early brain scanning have shown that feelings, empathy and emotional understanding are 'hard-wired' into children's brains through their early relationship experiences in the first years of life.

Attachment Theory and the role of the early years practitioner

Taking Bowlby's Attachment Theory, which focuses on children's experiences particularly in their first year of life, as a valid starting point, it follows that once children begin to feel emotionally secure in their early years setting, the scene is set for further learning to take place. Children therefore need to know that the setting is a place where emotions can be expressed. It is the ability to manage some of these emotions that is the challenge both for the individual child and the practitioner. Babies often develop a network of attachments made up of all the familiar people with whom they regularly come into contact with. It is the quality of such social experiences that is influential in the process of achieving healthy social and emotional development. One such familiar person is a baby's key person in their early years setting. A crucial factor in a child's social and emotional development, therefore, is the quality of social interactions between the early years practitioner as well as other children in the setting. To this end, the key person has a powerful impact on the wellbeing of their key children and their ability to develop and learn. Research has categorically shown that high-quality pre-school provision is significant in its positive effects on young children's

Plate 1 'Children's wellbeing is facilitated when interactions with adults are consistent, responsive, and sensitive'
Source: Elfer and Dearnley (2007: 267)

intellectual, social and emotional behaviour (Sylva *et al.*, 2010). Where practitioners are warm and responsive to children's individual needs, there will be better outcomes in terms of social and emotional behaviour. What this might mean for the early years practitioner in specific practical terms is covered in Chapter 3. However, the ability and willingness to respond with sensitivity when a baby is held, fed, talked to and soothed during daily interactions gives an overview of the foundation on which the early years practitioner must build.

Bowlby's Attachment Theory can be further looked at from the perspective of a behavioural system and as a developmental system.

1. Attachment as a behavioural system. Bowlby's theory suggests that all babies begin life with a specific behavioural system, the goal of which is to maintain close proximity to their caregiver. In stressful or uncertain situations, proximity to the caregiver gives reassurance; conversely, babies typically protest at separation from a preferred caregiver with whom they have established an attachment.

Behavioural tactics that babies use to 'keep an eye on' their caregiver

From birth to six months: tracking their caregiver's movements with their eyes, grasping, reaching, smiling and babbling to maintain the caregiver's attention. Six months onwards: following a caregiver they can see moving away, using the caregiver as a secure base from which to explore the environment.

2. Attachment as a developmental system. Bowlby portrayed parental sensitivity and a child's ability to trust the caregiver's accessibility to be at the root of their ability to develop a so-called 'healthy' personality. According to this element of his theory, specific parental behaviours are a determinant of babies' characteristic patterns of attachment. Four broad indices contribute to our understanding of sensitive parental behaviour:

    (a) Frequent and sustained physical contact between the parent and the baby, especially during the first six months, together with the parent's ability to soothe a distressed baby.

    (b) Sensitivity to the baby's signals, including responding appropriately.

    (c) An environment in which the baby can derive a sense of the consequences of their own actions.

    (d) The mutual delight that a parent and an infant find in each other's company.

Ainsworth and Wittig (1969) developed a study involving a so-called 'strange situation', designed to assess individual differences in one-year-old children's responses to familiar and unfamiliar caregivers. The study involved a series of short separations from, and reunions with, the parent in an unfamiliar room alongside a strange adult entering and leaving the room to assess the child's management of distress and the use of the parent as a secure base. Ainsworth and Wittig's findings led to three categories of attachment:

- Secure attachment, where babies use their parents as a secure base from which to explore. They may cry when their parents leave and actively greet their parents and seek contact during reunion.

- Avoidant attachment, characterised by babies who are usually not distressed when their parents leave the room and who react to the stranger in the same way as they do their parents. During reunion, they tend to avoid their parents and show minimal affective expression.

- Resistant attachment, where before separation babies seek closeness to their parents and often choose not to explore. When their parents return they sometimes display resistant behaviour, such as hitting or pushing, and often continue to cry after being picked up.

Ainsworth and Wittig (1969) further suggested the following hypotheses as a result of their 'strange situation' study: sensitive caregivers foster securely attached children; rejecting caregivers have avoidant children; and inconsistent caregivers tend to have resistant children. Avoidant children have parents who find it difficult to support their offspring with physical contact and who fail to understand their babies' perspective or respect their autonomy. Resistant attachment is associated with persistent parental unresponsiveness to the child and withdrawal of love as a means to control behaviour.

At-risk children

Ainsworth and Wittig's (1969) strange situation study has proved to be of seminal importance in the identification of at-risk children. To this end, a fourth category of attachment was added by Main and Solomon in 1990:

- Disorganised/disoriented attachment, where babies show a high level of insecurity. At reunion, these children engage in a variety of confused behaviours, such as looking away while being held by the parent or approaching with a dazed facial expression.

The subject of at-risk children is a difficult one for the dedicated early years practitioner to comprehend; however, at-risk children are a sad reality within the jurisdiction of early years practice. These are children who are, or who will be, an overt presence for some practitioners. With alarmingly high numbers of young children living in impoverished social and economic conditions (there were 4.1 million children, or 30%, living in poverty in the UK in 2017–18), researchers continue to examine the influence of persistent poverty on children's development.

Attachment Theory, emotional wellbeing and the early years setting

Elfer and Dearnley (2007: 267) argue that despite official endorsement of attachment principles in early years settings, these are often not translated into nursery practice; they cite multiple research studies spanning a decade that show that 'children's wellbeing is facilitated when interactions with adults are consistent, responsive, and sensitive'. The key person approach in early years settings, an approach in which one person assumes overall care and responsibility for a child, has been one such response to the need for consistency with childcare.

The key person approach: an overview

Babies and children under three thrive on consistency – for example, consistency of routine and of familiar places and patterns, both at home and in their early years setting. In line with Attachment Theory outlined above, consistency should extend to include regularity, predictability and constancy of relationships. A major element of provision of consistency within the early years environment can be offered through the key person approach. A key person is someone with whom the child can form a secure, trusting relationship. While in practice, many tasks within the setting may be shared by more than one person, the intention should be that as much as is feasible should be carried out by the key person. A key person is likely to assume overall responsibility for a group of key children. Noddings argues that 'we would all prefer to be cared for by someone who enjoys our company rather than by someone who acts out of grim duty' (2002: 178–179). Babies 'learn best by playing with the things they find in their world, and above all by playing with the familiar people who love them' (David et al., 2003: 150). Key persons should be practitioners who are experts in their field. They are specialists who understand and respond to babies' and young children's needs, both physical and emotional: specialists who can support developing social skills, who willingly interact with the children in their care and who share conversations fuelled by mutual enjoyment of genuinely shared interest. Specialist practitioners know how to develop the early years environment to support young children's individual needs.

Activity: linking theory to practice

Read through the overview of the key person approach and highlight explicit links to Attachment Theory.

The benefits of a key person approach

An effective key person approach supports the following benefits for babies and children under three:

1. Promoting healthy emotional attachments with a child by providing familiar, trusting, safe and secure relationships. The key person is the person who knows the child well and is aware of all the special details of how they are cared for, helping them to feel cherished and able to express themselves fully, to relax and feel confident that they matter and have value. The key person becomes the child's safe, secure and consistent base to return to, physically and emotionally.

2. Following and recognising the patterns, tones and rhythms of a child's life, thereby developing a deep understanding of their individual needs. The key person understands a child's current skills and interests and can engage them in and extend their play.

3. Establishing open communication with a child's parents to ensure the child's needs are met and planned for. The key person is the person who knows each child, their family and their circumstances, and is seen as someone who values what families want to say about their child. Conversely, parents are more likely to spend time talking to someone they feel is committed to caring for their child.

4. Acting as an advocate for the child, sharing with parents and other practitioners the specific interests and needs of their key children. The key person has a powerful impact on the wellbeing of their key children and their ability to develop and learn.

Outcomes for the setting of a key person approach will include improved care and learning for the children, and parents and families who are confident about leaving their children there.

Activity

1. Look through the benefits of a key person approach, above. Taking each of the four points in turn, discuss whether the children and families in your setting are benefitting optimally from your current organisational care systems.

   • How well does each key person know the children that they care for? What evidence is there within your setting to suggest the strength of relationships that exist? (You might wish to extend your discussions to paperwork such as observations, planning and recording.)

   • Ask each key person to identify one of the children in their care. How do they follow and recognise the patterns, tones and rhythms of each child's life?

   • How is open communication with parents established within your setting?

   • What does it mean to be an 'advocate for the child'?

2. Why will outcomes for the setting of a key person approach include improved care and learning for the children? Relate your answers to theory.

3. What are the implications for your setting, both in terms of current practice and changes you may have to make, and/or in terms of organisation?

Some issues to consider, based on Elfer and Dearnley's (2007) findings, include:

• How much of a priority is continuing professional development within your early years setting?

• Do key persons understand the need to work in partnership with *all* agencies involved with the child?

• Do key persons within the setting show a reluctance to develop close relationships with children that involve physical contact because of child protection concerns?

- Do hierarchical perceptions within your setting get in the way of quality provision? How high a status is placed on direct work with babies and children under three, where much physical care such as help with feeding or eating and supporting the development of independent learners is involved? Do your key persons derive status from administrative or organisational tasks rather than being involved in direct care of the children?

Measurement scales

Example 1. The Leuven Scale for Active Engagement in Learning

The Leuven Scale is a form of assessment developed by Professor Ferre Laevers (2005) and his team at Leuven University's Research Centre for Experiential Education (RCEE) in Belgium. The measurement tool focuses on two central indicators of quality early years provision: children's wellbeing and their involvement. Laevers' definition of wellbeing refers to children feeling at ease, being spontaneous and free of emotional tensions. Wellbeing, he argues, is crucial to good mental health. Wellbeing is also linked to self-confidence, high self-esteem and resilience. Involvement refers to being intensely engaged in activities and is considered to be a necessary condition for deep-level learning and development. Laevers has thus created a five-point scale to measure both wellbeing and involvement. In terms of measurement, a consistent low level of wellbeing and/or involvement means that it is likely a child's development will be threatened. The higher the levels of wellbeing and involvement that can be achieved for the child, the more the setting can add to the child's development. When there are high levels of wellbeing and involvement, deep- or optimum-level learning is taking place.

The evaluation process begins by assessing the levels of wellbeing and involvement using the scales outlined in Figure 2.1 below.

Wellbeing level	Wellbeing signals
1. Extremely low	The child clearly shows signs of discomfort such as crying or screaming. They may look dejected, sad, frightened or angry. The child does not respond to the environment, avoids contact and is withdrawn. The child may behave aggressively, hurting themselves or others.
2. Low	The posture, facial expression and actions indicate that the child does not feel at ease. However, the signals are less explicit than under level 1, or the sense of discomfort is not expressed the whole time.
3. Moderate	The child has a neutral posture. Facial expression and posture show little or no emotion. There are no signs indicating sadness or pleasure, comfort or discomfort.
4. High	The child shows obvious signs of satisfaction (as listed under level 5). However, these signals are not constantly present with the same intensity.
5. Extremely high	The child looks happy and cheerful, smiles, cries out with pleasure. They may be lively and full of energy. Actions can be spontaneous and expressive. The child may talk to themselves, play with sounds, hum, sing. The child appears relaxed and does not show any signs of stress or tension. They are open and accessible to the environment. The child expresses self-confidence and self-assurance.

Involvement level	Involvement signals
1. Extremely low	Activity is simple, repetitive and passive. The child seems absent and displays no energy. They may stare into space or look around to see what others are doing.
2. Low	Frequently interrupted activity. The child will be engaged in the activity for some of the time they are observed, but there will be moments of non-activity when they will stare into space, or be distracted by what is going on around.

Figure 2.1 The Leuven Scales for Wellbeing and Involvement

Involvement level	Involvement signals
3. Moderate	Mainly continuous activity. The child is busy with the activity but at a fairly routine level and there are few signs of real involvement. They make some progress with what they are doing but don't show much energy and concentration and can be easily distracted.
4. High	Continuous activity with intense moments. The child's activity has intense moments and at all times they seem involved. They are not easily distracted.
5. Extremely high	The child shows continuous and intense activity revealing the greatest involvement. They are concentrated, creative, energetic and persistent throughout nearly all the observed period.

Figure 2.1 Cont.

Practitioners should observe babies and children as a group or individually for approximately two minutes, then give a score for wellbeing and involvement. Where children are observed to be operating at less than a score of 4 or 5, learning will be limited. However, it is useful to observe how well practitioners tune in to the children's levels of wellbeing and involvement and respond to low levels sensitively. Even a low level of wellbeing or involvement can become a learning opportunity which can result in higher levels. The initial observation is the starting point for further analysis, concentrating on children displaying lower levels of wellbeing and involvement. This analysis supports practitioners to reflect on the quality of the provision, including providing some clues about how to support individual children. Measuring children's levels of wellbeing and involvement can also empower and energise practitioners, when their high-quality provision and interactions enable children to demonstrate higher levels of wellbeing and involvement more consistently.

Ten action points

The RCEE formulated a list of ten action points that enable practitioners to identify strategies for ensuring the learning environment (both physical and emotional) supports children's well-being and involvement:

1. Organise the physical learning environment in attractive and distinct corners or areas.
2. Review the resources within the areas and ensure there is a level of challenge for all children, including the most able.
3. Introduce new and unconventional materials and experiences.
4. Observe and identify children's interests and offer experiences that respond to these interests.
5. Support activities by stimulating inputs.
6. Widen the possibilities for free initiative and support them with sound agreements.
7. Improve the quality of the relations among children and between children and teacher(s).
8. Introduce activities that help children to explore the world of behaviour, feelings and values.
9. Identify children with emotional problems and work out sustaining interventions.
10. Identify children with developmental needs and work out interventions that engender involvement.

In addition to the action points, Professor Ferre Laevers (director of the RCEE) highlights the importance of the way in which adults interact with children. He believes that this is key to the achievement of wellbeing and involvement. Laevers (1994) describes it in the following terms:

> Stimulating interventions are open impulses that engender involvement, such as: suggesting activities to children, inviting children to communicate, asking thought-provoking questions and giving rich information. Sensitivity is evidenced in responses that witness empathic understanding of the child. Giving autonomy means: respecting the children's initiative, acknowledging their interests, giving them room for experimentation, letting them decide upon the way an activity is performed and letting them participate in the setting of rules.

Example 2. The United Kingdom: the Sustained Shared Thinking and Emotional Wellbeing (SSTEW) scales (for children aged between two and five years old)

The SSTEW scales (Siraj *et al.*, 2015) consider practices that support children aged between two and five years of age in developing skills in sustained shared thinking and emotional wellbeing, as well as developing strong relationships, effective communication and aspects of self-regulation. For this reason, it is useful to include this scale when considering the children in our care aged between two and three years old. The SSTEW scales focus on the pedagogy within the setting, the adult's role in supporting children's learning and development, and the quality of interactions with and between children. The scales need to be used by practitioners with knowledge of child development and appropriate practice. Note that before using the SSTEW scales for professional development, the authors strongly suggest that you attend a bespoke training session.

Five scales are used to assess the quality of children's interactions:

1. Building trust, confidence and independence.
2. Social and emotional wellbeing.
3. Supporting and extending language and communication.
4. Supporting learning and critical thinking.
5. Assessing learning and language.

There are seven levels from inadequate to excellent, for a total of 14 items under the five scales. In brief, each item is rated from 1 to 7, using three observations as evidence. The average scores are then calculated to give a rating. The five-scale ratings can be entered onto a 'scale profile' that gives a visual representation of the seven levels, so practitioners can see at a glance those areas that need further work or those that are doing really well. As with other similar quality assessment scales, there are examples and supplementary information sections for each item. Have a look at the sub-scale for social and emotional wellbeing here:

Item 4: supporting socio-emotional wellbeing (Siraj et al., 2015: 20)

Inadequate 1

1.1 Feelings expressed by the children are played down, ignored, dismissed or ridiculed.

1.2 Staff do not display a warm and welcoming body language to the children.

1.3 Staff do not lay out the setting or organise activities to encourage social interaction.

Minimal 3

3.1 Staff empathise with the children and help them to deal with feelings expressed.

3.2 Staff encourage children to play alongside each other providing additional toys/props and resources to support continued play. As the children progress to playing together, staff support them in helping each other and sharing.

3.3 Positive individual attention is paid to most children at some point during the session.

3.4 Staff are warm, friendly and calm. They use calming gestures, physical proximity, pats and hugs when necessary and appropriate.

Good 5

5.1 Children are encouraged to express/say what they feel and need.

5.2 Planning shows evidence of learning intentions that are designed to support social interaction, including encouraging collaborative activities and play where appropriate.

5.3 Children are encouraged to seek an adult's support when sharing or playing breaks down.

5.4 Staff are responsive to the children's needs, feelings and moods. They may play, show liveliness and have fun with the children supporting positive emotions.

Excellent 7

7.1 Staff provide opportunities for children to talk about feelings and needs – often using the children's own experiences. They may use stories or props, e.g. 'Puppet misses his family; how shall we make him feel better?'

7.2 Children are asked to show or say what they can understand from the non-verbal expressions of others in the group, from story books, photos, DVDs, etc.

7.3 Staff support children in communicating with and recognising and responding to the feelings of others, including where children may have difficulty expressing their needs or wants.

7.4 Staff look beyond the child to explain their feelings, making changes within the environment/routine, etc. when necessary.

For personal reflection

Reading through Item 4, what might observations of your own practice reveal?

Example 3. Germany: Positive Entwicklung und Resilienz im Kindergartenalltag (PERIK)

PERIK (Mayr and Ulich, 2009) is an empirically based instrument for practitioners to use to observe and assess pre-school children's wellbeing in early childhood settings. A strong theoretical background underpins its development, including research on mental health and resilience. Resilience research has tended to focus on children who may be considered at-risk: children who grow up in particularly difficult conditions and who therefore often suffer from difficulties in later childhood and/or later life. There are, however, a proportion of children who grow up in particularly difficult conditions, but who become successful and happy either in later childhood and/or later life; it is these children who Mayr and Ulich (2009) describe as 'resilient'. As a result of their approach, PERIK was developed on the basis of a concept of wellbeing as 'eudemonic' (one that emphasises optimum development of an individual's intrinsic potential) and incorporates a common core of six dimensions of social-emotional wellbeing that underpin the foundations for positive development. These are: (1) making contact/social performance; (2) self-control/thoughtfulness; (3) self-assertiveness; (4) emotional stability/coping with stress; (5) task orientation; and (6) pleasure in exploration. PERIK's six scales are outlined below along with 'competencies' or criteria developed for each area:

1. Making contact/social performance
   a. Where the child makes contact easily with their peers.
   b. Where the child initiates games that appeal to their peers.
   c. Where the child knows how to join in with other children in play.
   d. Where the child's opinion is respected among their peers.
   e. Where the child has friendships among their peers.

2. Self-control/thoughtfulness
   a. Where the child can wait for a turn.
   b. Where the child respects the boundaries and needs of other children.
   c. Where the child is worried if they think they have hurt another child, for example, who apologises and tries to make up.
   d. Where the child has respect and empathy for the feelings of adults.
   e. Where the child respects 'dos' and 'don'ts' within the setting.
   f. Where the child can be glad for other children, sharing their joy and success.

3. Self-assertiveness
   a. Where the child enjoys talking about their experiences.
   b. Where the child will speak up for themselves if they do not feel an adult has treated them fairly.

   c. Where the child will speak up for themselves if they do not feel another child has treated them fairly or in a way that is acceptable to them.

   d. Where the child can defend themselves either physically or verbally when 'attacked' by other children.

   e. Where the child does not allow themselves to be put under pressure, for example, if they hold an opinion that others do not share.

4. Emotional stability/coping with stress
   a. Where the child is able to self-regulate their emotions.
   b. Where the child appears well-balanced.
   c. Where the child does not mind too much if they make a mistake or lose at a game.

And on the negative end of this dimension:

   d. Where the child takes a long time to recover after stress and excitement.

   e. Where the child quickly loses their confidence and is easily stressed.

5. Task orientation
   a. Where the child quickly settles to a task.
   b. Where the child works on a task independently.
   c. Where the child works quickly.
   d. Where the child works carefully and precisely.
   e. Where the child can concentrate on one thing for a relatively long period of time.

   And on the negative end of this dimension:

   f. Where the child needs praise and encouragement to finish a task.

6. Pleasure in exploring
   a. Where the child likes to explore new things.
   b. Where the child is optimistic and positive when beginning something new.

    c. Where the child asks questions and wants to know about things.

    d. Where the child explores new things independently.

    e. Where the child gives themselves time to become familiar with new situations and things.

    f. Where the child will try things that seem difficult or at which they might not succeed.

It is important to note that the items in PERIK listed above relate to competencies or concrete learning goals incorporated within many German early years curricula. At the same time, there is scope for making connections across early years curricula from other countries.

Activity

How do the six PERIK socio-emotional areas of wellbeing outlined above map to the personal, social and emotional elements of the early years framework that you work within? Take one area at a time. Would you wish to add anything to the competencies listed under each area? Justify your responses.

Mayr and Ulich (2009) argue that PERIK has the potential to support the early years practitioner to understand and attune to individual children, thus providing scope for specific support and learning opportunities in the area of personal, social and emotional development to be planned for and further evaluated. They further argue that outcomes include discovery, such as a child who appears to have a lot of contact with other children, but who only rarely takes the initiative and is not necessarily interacting with their peers successfully, thus providing scope for specific intervention and support from the early years practitioner. Consider the following two case studies which describe very different scenarios, yet which reveal much about personal, social and emotional wellbeing in reaction to each child.

Case study 1: Jemima

At just three years old, Jemima had recently moved house from one part of the country to another. She was an only child and both her parents worked long hours. She spent most of the day with Sarah, her nanny, and usually saw her parents only briefly each evening.

Following detailed observations of her movements during the course of a session early on after her arrival at the setting, it became evident to her key person that, although Jemima was regularly visiting different areas of the setting, she was doing so as an observer rather than as a participant. She would only play with a resource if no one else was using it. If another child came along and tried to talk to her, she would walk away. Further, if her key person was focusing on a particular activity with one or more children, Jemima would often try to draw the key person's attention away from the other children by making a statement such as, 'When I woke up this morning I shouted, "Mummy! Mummy!" but guess what? Mummy didn't come! Sarah came upstairs and helped me get up'.

It became apparent that Jemima had found the house move difficult and was unsettled by it. She talked about the fact that she had lived in a large house before, but now she lived in an 'enormous' house. She missed her parents. Jemima was able to express how she was feeling. At the same time, while what she was saying was not inappropriate, the context of the situation was a concern to setting staff.

As a result of a discussion between key persons in the setting, the following plan of action was agreed. Jemima would be given time to talk with her key person about her new routines at home. She would then be helped and supported to understand that these routines were permanent. In addition to addressing the issue, this would give her some of the individual attention she needed. The key person would invite Jemima's parents to come in for a progress report. Positives would be discussed, such as their daughter's use of language and her artwork, to provide a balance to the consultation which would also serve to raise her parents' awareness of her insecurity. A series of adult-focused activities involving the older children working in groups would be planned over the period of a month. Jemima would then experience being part of a group with adult support on a regular basis. If Jemima was spending time with her key person in the setting, for example, listening to a story, the key person would invite another child to come and listen too. Jemima would then come to understand that other children needed, and indeed were entitled to, her key person's time and attention as well. Comments would be made by the key person, such as 'Who can we invite to come and listen to the story with us?' Should Jemima be introduced to another child by her key person and start to play alongside them, her key person would subtly withdraw and leave them to play together. Names were important to Jemima, so it was agreed that all key persons would introduce Jemima to other children she was with and vice versa.

As a result of the action plan, Jemima gradually needed to talk about home life less and less. Being given the opportunity to talk things through each day, with an adult who she knew would listen to her, helped her to work through her unsettled feelings to ones of understanding and acceptance. Jemima's parents appreciated greatly the key person's time and obvious care for their daughter. Her mother started to go to work later one day a week so that she could drop Jemima off at the nursery and her father came home early twice a week so that he could pick her up. Sometimes he would try to work from home. Jemima became more and more relaxed in the company of her peers. She started to enjoy their company. At first she relied on her key person inviting her to join in with small groups, indicating her willingness to be asked by standing close and trying to make eye contact with her. She no longer tried to draw her attention away from other children.

Jemima loved stories. Soon she was inviting children to join her being read to without any support from her key person in the setting. Jemima eventually became confident enough to introduce herself to children whose names she was not sure of. One day, she wanted to play in the water tray alongside a peer. 'My name is Jemima', she said. 'What are you called?' When the boy did not reply, she put her hands on her hips, leaned towards him, ensuring she made eye contact with him, and said, 'You're supposed to tell me your name now!' By the end of her first term, Jemima would greet her key person only briefly when she entered the setting, preferring to seek out the company of her peers straight away. She started to regularly invite one or two special friends to her home to play and to have tea.

Case study 2: Alastair

Alastair, aged two years and four months, was observed as he played outside in the garden of the Children's Centre he attended for 15 hours a week. An activity had been set up for the three-year-old children at the setting to access, involving finding eggs hidden in straw, placing them in a basket and counting them. The early years practitioner who had set up the activity had also provided a large whiteboard positioned at child height, with an egg number line from 1 to 20 attached to the outer edge and large, thick whiteboard pens. Children who came to explore the activity were encouraged to record the number of eggs they had found on the whiteboard once they had counted them. The early years practitioner supported the children to find the corresponding number on the egg number line, modelling one-to-one ordination from left to right. Alastair was intrigued by the activity and observed it from a distance for about 15 minutes. Then, as soon as he saw an opportunity, he went straight to the whiteboard and counted out loud to seven, while simultaneously (albeit randomly) pointing to eggs on the number line with his left hand and making a mark for every number he spoke out loud with the pen he held in his right. The numbers that Alastair had written as he counted appeared on the board as no more than a series of regimented, squiggly lines. In his own mind, however, and from the perspective of the observer of the scenario, Alastair had written his own set of numbers from 1 to 7. He wrote them from left to right on the board before moving away from the activity. The practitioner did not interact with him at all, because he was only aged two, and the activity had been designed for the three-year-olds at the setting.

Activity

Map the six PERIK socio-emotional areas of wellbeing, first to Jemima's case and then to Alastair's. If you are approaching this activity as a staff team, it might be sensible to divide into two groups, each looking at one individual case study together before sharing as a whole group. Look at the criteria developed for each area:

1. Making contact/social performance.
2. Self-control/thoughtfulness.
3. Self-assertiveness.
4. Emotional stability/coping with stress.
5. Task orientation.
6. Pleasure in exploring.

Make an initial judgement about each child and then rate their progress in each area following intervention by their key person and other staff at the setting. Would you have done anything else for Jemima or Alastair in relation to supporting their wellbeing? It might be helpful to revisit the second point for reflective activity from Chapter 1.

Developing self-regulation in the under threes: learning for the future

From about the age of a year to 18 months, children start, with support, to be able to control their urges – or in other words, they will begin to learn to evaluate what they see, hear, touch, taste and smell, comparing their experiences to what they already know. In addition, they will perhaps even do some of the things that you ask them to do! This is the beginning of self-regulation. It is important to remember that just because a child responds to a request once, it does not necessarily mean that they will always respond in the same way or automatically do everything you ask them to do; however, it is a start – a step in the right direction in terms of cognitive development and the ability to think through a scenario before they decide how to act. The beginnings of self-regulation at this age lay important foundations for the child's future when they will need the right skills to develop friendships and play happily with friends, for example, or to function in school and under-stand how to respond to and respect the adult relationships in their lives, such as with parents and carers. There are essentially two sides to self-regulation from the perspective of the young child. These are:

1. The 'dos', which include doing things or finishing things that they would prefer not to, such as coming inside for a nappy change when they are engrossed in creating a wonderful mud pie in the garden, but it is simply too unhygienic (and unpleasant!) to continue doing so with a full nappy.

2. The 'don'ts', where the child stops themselves from doing something they think they would rather do, such as touching a hot oven or a nettle in the garden (linking in with young children's natural curiosity to experience and explore the world around them, particularly through the sense of touch).

Most children find it easier to respond to 'don'ts' than 'dos', perhaps because it takes more mental effort to force themselves to do something they would rather not do than to stop doing something that is fun, intriguing and exciting.

Self-regulation and wellbeing

It is important for the early years practitioner to consider the development of self-regulation alongside a child's wellbeing, because understanding how to follow directions and behave in adult–child and peer–peer situations is something that all children need to learn in order to function well in their families and cultures (Galinsky, 2010). Self-regulation involves learning how to navigate the world safely, thus supporting and contributing to a child's overall sense of wellbeing, and their knowing and understanding right from wrong. Blair and Diamond (2008, cited in Florez, 2011: 47) argue that 'self-regulation is clearly not an isolated skill. Children must translate what they experience into information they can use to regulate thoughts, emotions, and behaviours'. Self-regulation therefore incorporates elements of Pollard and Lee's (2003) domains of child wellbeing, particularly cognitive and emotional.

Self-regulation, babies and children under three: the role of the early years practitioner

Eventually, most children will be able to routinely self-regulate without adult assistance; in other words, they will have internalised self-regulation. Lev Vygotsky described internalisation as a process which children progress from co-regulating behaviour with an adult to being able to do so independently; thus, to develop self-regulation skills, children need many opportunities to experience and practise with their early carers. Florez (2011) argues that scaffolding is essential to help young children develop self-regulation skills. In this respect, it is useful to think of Vygotsky's zone of proximal development where a child's learning is developed and supported through the involvement of a more experienced other, often an adult. Social interaction with a more competent member of society enables knowledge to be transmitted to an individual who, in turn, is able to internalise and incorporate new ideas and concepts into their existing repertoire. In the role of a more experienced other, the effective early years practitioner will use a variety of strategies to help bridge the developmental space between what children already know and are capable of, and what they need to or could move on to next. They will:

1. Use cues. Cues from the early years practitioner, such as speaking soothingly to babies and young children and using a soothing touch, translate into cues for them that support the development of self-calming skills. A distressed baby is not experiencing emotional wellbeing, nor is a two-year-old child crying in the middle of a play area or who does not want to leave the parent or carer in the morning; discovering and helping to soothe the cause of distress is therefore essential. The skilled early years practitioner is someone who knows how to listen and respond to this age group and how to understand the reason for their unhappiness – is it tiredness, for example? Does the baby need to be rocked to sleep? Are they hungry? The two- and three-year-old children in your setting will translate cues from the practitioner, such as 'Your turn is next', into self-regulation skills that help them not to give in to urges to grab food or toys. They come to understand that they will always have their turn to eat and to play with the toys that interest and excite them, thus helping them to regulate emotional tension. It is important to understand that self-regulation skills develop gradually, and the early years practitioner must therefore hold developmentally appropriate expectations for children's behaviour.

2. Model. By demonstrating appropriate behaviour or actions, the early years practitioner will model how to accomplish a task and use the self-regulation needed to complete it. They may, for example, model appropriate language and social skills: 'We will give teddy back to James now because he was playing with it, wasn't he? Well done! Let's see what else we can find to play with'. Sharing a book models how to turn the pages gently and with care, looking with interest at the contents that depict

everyday scenarios the young child can relate to and that are therefore meaningful. There are books that are suitable even for babies and that will stimulate their interest, such as the Ladybird 'Baby Touch' series.

3. Allow increasing independence through gradual withdrawal of support. Being able to scaffold children's learning and development gradually involves knowing when to withdraw support. Children in the birth to three years age range are unlikely to develop overall consistency of self-regulation skills, therefore careful monitoring of progress is essential. There will be times, however, when progress will be made: walking with support to walking unaided, for example, or wearing nappies to being fully toilet trained.

The early years practitioner does therefore play a crucial role in supporting babies and children under three to develop foundational self-regulation skills. Because this is such an important role, it demands knowledge and understanding of the age range, particularly from a developmental perspective. The skilled early years practitioner will be able to watch for, and identify, opportunities on a daily basis to scaffold self-regulation, monitoring progress through observation and planning to ensure success.

 ## Chapter conclusion

Chapter 2 has explored approaches to understanding and measuring children's personal, social and emotional wellbeing in some depth. Attachment Theory is considered as an appropriate umbrella theory when considering the needs of babies in particular. The chapter further considers measurement of wellbeing through means of observation and rating scales established in research. Theory links with practice in relation to the role of the early years practitioner working with this age group. The notion of self-regulation is also discussed, making links with cognitive and emotional wellbeing.

Resources for further exploration

Laevers, F. (1994) *The Leuven Involvement Scale for Young Children*. Manual and Video. Experiential Education Series, No. 1. Leuven, Belgium: Research Centre for Experiential Education, Leuven University.

Laevers, F. (2005) (ed.) *Well-being and Involvement in Care Settings. A Process-oriented Self-evaluation Instrument.* Leuven, Belgium: Research Centre for Experiential Education, Leuven University.

Mayr, T. and Ulich, M. (2009) Social-emotional well-being and resilience of children in early childhood settings – PERIK: an empirically based observation scale for practitioners. *Early Years*, 29 (1): 45–57.

Siraj, I., Kingston, D. and Melhuish, E. (2015) *Sustained Shared Thinking and Emotional Well-being (SSTEW) Scale for 2–5-year-olds Provision.* London: Trentham IOE Press.

For a range of up-to-date articles, research papers, reports and information on wellbeing from a global perspective, visit: www.oecd.org/statistics/measuring-well-being-and-progress.htm

For a short, clear explanation of self-regulation in young children, visit: www.pacey.org.uk/news-and-views/pacey-blog/july-2019/keep-calm-lets-talk-about-self-regulation/

Wellbeing, the early years practitioner and the early years setting

Leadership matters

Since there is only space for a brief overview of the importance of strong leadership within the early years setting, the aim here is to establish a definitive link between leadership style and setting wellbeing. International research in the field shows, for example, a significant correlation between effective leadership and the quality of early years services (Siraj-Blatchford and Manni, 2011). While key national studies have provided substantial empirical evidence for the important role of early years leaders in effecting change and making a difference in the lives of young children and families, effective team leading fundamentally supports strong staff morale and a clear, collaborative vision. Early years leaders' attitudes and team-leading strategies have the capacity to strongly influence pedagogical orientations along with the self-confidence of teams in their pedagogical work, and thus pedagogical quality. Thus, Male and Nicholson (2016: 319) argue that 'a key aspect of formal leadership in early childhood education and care … is the recognition of the potential capability of other actors in the system to make a positive contribution to the setting'. Additionally, Moyles (2006) suggests that leadership in early childhood education and care has to be a collective effort that is child-centred, and which provides the basis of the ways in which practitioners work with children and families.

Strehmal (2016) identifies human resource management as a core aspect of effective early years leadership. The goals of human resource management are twofold: on the one hand, it is important to reach and strengthen pedagogical quality and provide excellent learning opportunities for the children. On the other hand, it is the responsibility of leaders to care for the professional development of the staff as well as to ensure job satisfaction, work ability and health of every person working in the institution. Beside the tasks of educational leadership and personnel management, leaders are responsible for work conditions and quality development. Utilising these practices, they should want to promote motivation, learning and participation of the pedagogical staff as prerequisites for good pedagogical quality as well as for professional development, wellbeing and health. Strehmal (2016) also considers the importance of self-management; leaders often have a large amount of autonomy to organise their work, which means that they alone are responsible for their own working structures and time schedules. However, self-management is more than that; it also means to care for one's own wellbeing, health and professional development.

A reflective activity for setting leaders

How are you? Write an honest account. Use the following points.

- Would you describe yourself as happy? Fulfilled? Content?
- Do you like your job?
- How well do you think you are doing as a leader?
- Do you have aspirations for your setting and for the staff team that work within it? What are these, and why?
- What is your current focus at work? How useful is this in relation to your own and others' wellbeing? Does it support the future of the setting within the context of the notion of Moyles' (2006) 'collective effort'?

Keep your notes in mind as you read further on into the chapter.

The impact of individual staff wellbeing on the care environment

A recent publication from the Pre-School Learning Alliance called *Minds Matter: The Impact of Working in the Early Years Sector on Practitioners' Mental Health and Wellbeing* (2018) reports the findings of a survey undertaken across the early years sector, which highlight mental health and wellbeing as a current focus for serious consideration. The survey was conducted online between 23 April and 18 May 2018, and received 2,039 responses. Respondents comprised of pre-schools (43%), nurseries (27%), childminders (15%) and a small number of primary school nursery classes (3%), Children's Centres (2%), maintained nursery schools (1%), nannies (1%) and out-of-hours school clubs (1%). Note: one survey question on working outside of hours was asked differently depending on whether the respondent effectively paid themselves a wage (i.e. setting owners and childminders) or were paid members of staff: the former were asked how often they work outside of what they consider 'reasonable hours', while the latter were asked how often they work outside of paid hours. Key findings were as follows:

- 25% of respondents were considering leaving the early years sector due to stress or mental health difficulties;
- 66% of respondents said their personal relationships have been negatively affected by work-related stress or mental health difficulties over the past year;
- 62% of (non-self-employed) respondents worked outside of paid working hours 'very often', with a further 19% working outside of paid working hours 'quite often';
- 62% of respondents did not think their work life and non-work life were balanced;
- 44% of respondents had felt stressed about work or an issue relating to work in the last month 'very often', and a further 30% 'quite often';
- the top four sources of stress identified by respondents were: 1. administration and paperwork; 2. financial resources of the setting; 3. workload (other than administration and paperwork); and 4. pay;
- fatigue (60%), loss of motivation (58%), anxiety (57%) and insomnia (53%) were the most commonly cited symptoms/health impacts experienced due to work, or where work was a contributing factor cited by respondents;
- 52% of respondents have not spoken to anyone at work about their stress or mental health issues.

Personal wellbeing within the early years setting can thus be looked at as a type of equation, in that it is determined by the interaction between the setting (or working) environment, the nature of the work being undertaken, and the response of the individual practitioner. To this end, personal wellbeing can

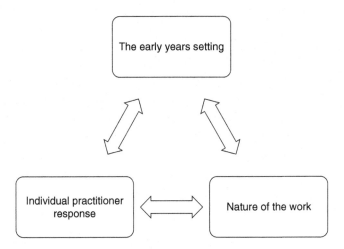

Figure 3.1 The relationship between the working environment and the early years
practitioner

also be looked at along a two-way continuum where key factors regarding the workplace constantly impact on the individual (see Figure 3.1). Promoting the mental wellbeing of employees can yield benefits for the early years setting, such as increased commitment, job satisfaction, staff performance and retention. Studies have additionally shown that contentment at work results in reduced staff absenteeism.

Work has an important role in promoting individual mental wellbeing and is an important determinant of self-esteem and identity, providing a sense of fulfilment and opportunities for social interaction (National Institute for Health and Clinical Excellence, 2009: 6). However, a perceived imbalance on the part of the early years practitioner between the effort required and the rewards of the job they are required to undertake can lead to unhappiness and has the potential to become a source of disharmony between the practitioner and the setting. In a worst-case scenario, such a perceived imbalance can even lead to stress, both on the part of the practitioner, who may as a result need time off work to recover, and on the part of the setting, with a resulting strain on other members of staff who must fill in, thus disrupting their own personal work routines. A sense of injustice and unfairness arising from management processes can also have the same potential effect, and it is to this end that setting leaders must consider their personal approach as to what constitutes successful management.

The care and learning environment in early years settings should be one that is developed with the unique and specific needs of babies and children under three in mind. The care and learning environment includes those adults who work within it. They are caring for an age group with unique characteristics, who behave in certain ways and who have specialised needs; if the principal need for newborn babies is that of calm, for example, then a setting characterised by staff dissatisfaction and/or disharmony will not support this underlying need.

Working as a team

> Successful [settings] encourage co-ordination by creating collaborative environ-
> ments which encourage involvement, professional development, mutual support
> and assistance in problem solving.
>
> (Hopkins *et al.*, 1996, cited in Harris, 2002: 55)

In early years childcare, a team is a group of people who work together to meet the aims of their establishment or setting. Because most early years workers are required to work alongside colleagues in a team, effective professionals working in the field of early years therefore need to be skilled in, and to understand the nature of, collaborative practice – the ability to work with others from different professions and perspectives. Early years work is people-based, highly dependent on interpersonal relationships and shared values. In order to function well as a team, members must be:

- motivated towards common goals;
- provided with the support and encouragement necessary to achieve these goals;
- able to communicate effectively.

Nias *et al.* (1989) further explored organisational culture, and identified five key aspects:

- beliefs and values;
- understandings;
- attitudes;
- meanings and norms;
- symbols, rituals and ceremonies (for example, bringing in cake on your birthday, or going out as a staff for a Christmas meal).

Factors that get in the way of creating an effective working culture can include the following (Nias et al., 1989: 11):

- The building that people work in (e.g. making excuses such as 'It's not conducive to practice exemplified in the curriculum' or 'We just don't have the space', as opposed to creatively making the most of the space available. How to make the most of available space within your early years setting is explored in *Appropriate Environments for Children under Three*, book 1 of this series).

- The organisational arrangements of the setting, such as different break times for members of staff, meaning that it can be difficult to find time to come together as a team.

- The time given for working and communicating together. Teams need time to plan together, for example, or to discuss certain children. It is important to be aware of and take into account factors such as these.

- The personal inclinations (including attitudes to work) of the individuals involved.

- The traditions attached to ways of working, which may for example result in inflexibility on the part of individual practitioners and can include more extreme behaviour, such as defending one's perceived 'territory' and sending out challenging or aggressive non-verbal gestures to others.

In order to work effectively within a team, early years practitioners need to have a panoply of skills at their disposal, including the ability to communicate and to negotiate; the ability to be flexible, reactive and responsive; and the ability to reflect and evaluate both at an individual and a team level.

Activity: working as a team 1

1. What other skills would you add to the ones outlined above?
2. Why is it necessary to have those skills in order to be able to work successfully as part of a team?
3. Why is it necessary to be able to reflect and evaluate both at an individual and a team level?

Activity: working as a team 2

Putting the story in order

Note: this activity will need a little preparation by the setting leader. You will need to copy a children's picture book of your choice onto A3 paper (make sure you choose a book that does not include page numbers).

In groups of up to 12 (an average staff-size meeting group):

1. Give each member of the group a double-page spread from the children's picture book. The spread must not be shared with colleagues.

2. Through discussion, the group must ascertain in which order the pages go to make up the complete story.

3. *Only* when they have made their final decision as a group can they reveal their spreads and put them together *in that order*.

4. Some discussion may then ensue as to whether the spreads would benefit from any re-ordering.

5. Now members discuss as a group the way they approached the task. Using large pieces of paper, they record the characteristics of the decision-making process. (Note: make sure the group records the decision-making process such as listening to others and taking turns to talk, rather than the process of putting a story in the correct sequence. This exercise is about effectively communicating to reach an agreed decision.)

6. Map the outcomes of the exercise to staff decision-making processes and effective communication within the setting. Depending on the text(s) you choose you may find the following:

    *   sometimes the solution to the issue or problem is straightforward and everyone can readily agree;

    *   sometimes it takes time to reach a decision because there are many elements to consider and discuss before an agreement can be made;

    *   sometimes decisions have to be made going on the information/resources that you have. You may not feel you have all the information or resources you would like, but nevertheless a

decision must be made within the parameters set by what you do have available. This category maps well to issues such as optimum use of resources, including individual members of staff, and space availability.

Supporting individual wellbeing

The National Institute for Health and Clinical Excellence (2017) states that employees should be managed by people who support their health and wellbeing. The body suggests adopting an organisation-wide approach to promoting the wellbeing of all employees through working in partnership with them. It argues that this approach should integrate the promotion of wellbeing into all policies and practices concerned with leading people, including those related to employment rights and working conditions. Within their early years settings, leaders should therefore seek to:

- promote a culture of participation, equality and fairness that is based on open communication and inclusion;
- adopt a leadership style that encourages participation, delegation, constructive feedback, mentoring and coaching;
- motivate employees and provide them with the training and support they need to develop their performance and job satisfaction;
- identify and respond with sensitivity to employees' emotional concerns and symptoms of mental health problems, including understanding when it is necessary to refer an employee to occupational health services or other sources of help and support.

In addition, leaders should endeavour to increase their understanding of how leadership style and practices can help to promote the wellbeing of employees and keep their stress to a minimum. To this end, it is a good idea to develop a wellbeing policy within the setting in recognition of the fact that the staff team is its most important resource.

Staff should be valued through personal and professional support, involvement in setting decision-making and through access to professional development. All wellbeing activities should be focused on everybody being able to work together to improve their working conditions, and this should be achievable within a 'no-blame' environment. Leaders should therefore develop the following within their settings:

- regular opportunities to allow staff to discuss wellbeing issues;
- a range of strategies for involving staff in setting decision-making processes, for example, during regular staff meetings, and including opportunities to review and share effective practice;
- regular reviews of communication systems to ensure staff are well informed;
- appraisal systems linked to clear job descriptions (thus establishing clear roles and goals for development);
- additional support in particularly stressful times, including responding sensitively and flexibly to external pressures which impact on staff lives;
- ensuring staff have knowledge of and access to union representation;
- regular reviews of the demands on staff time to see if things can be done differently;
- work towards a positive setting ethos where everyone feels valued;
- work towards a positive staff–children relationship, to ensure both an effective care and learning environment and a happy, harmonious place to work for both staff and the children in their care.

 ## Wellbeing and the role of the individual practitioner

In addition to acknowledging the setting's responsibility to practitioner wellbeing, practitioners must be encouraged to take the primary responsibility for their own health and wellbeing. This involves taking care of oneself through developing individual self-awareness, knowing when the boundaries of cope-ability are being stretched and letting the setting leader know, through procedures set up specifically for this kind of communication, about any aspect of work or the working environment that may be affecting health or, indeed, external factors that may be impacting on performance within the setting. Early intervention where support can be factored in straightaway is far better than trying to soldier on alone and suffering needlessly.

Activity

Ask yourself the following questions. Be as honest with yourself as you can; no one else will be reading your responses.

1. How healthy is my lifestyle? Is there anything I can do to change it for the better? (Eating more fruit and vegetables, for example.)

2. How is my physical health? Do I need to find more support for how I am feeling physically? (Always find time to see a doctor or talk to your setting leader about adjustments to your working pattern as a result of physical ill-health.)

3. Does anything restrict my performance at work? Am I worrying about something nearly all of the time? Do I need to tell someone at work about a personal issue that I may need support with?

4. What one small change could I make to my lifestyle that would improve my sense of wellbeing? (Walking or cycling to work instead of taking the car, for example.)

An observation tool: the Adult Engagement Scale

Bertram and Pascal (1996) developed the Adult Engagement Scale as part of their Effective Early Learning (EEL) project. The Adult Engagement Scale is an observation tool designed to look at practitioner behaviour, and is built on the premise that it is the *quality* of practitioner interactions with young children that is critical in determining the effectiveness of educational provision. Bertram and Pascal argue that it is the interactions between the practitioner and the child that are the important factor in the effectiveness of the learning experience. The tool measures three aspects of the adult's behaviour that affect the child's learning – sensitivity, stimulation and autonomy. Bertram and Pascal's research showed that adult sensitivity to children is a basic precondition for educative interactions to occur; stimulation occurs once a level of sensitivity and responsiveness between adults and children has been established. The Adult Engagement Scale (Figure 3.2) is still available for use within early years settings and may be a tool for the setting to consider using to support both individual self-reflection and professional

Adult Engagement Observation Sheet
Observer…
Date…
Observing…
Total number of children present…
Total number of adults present…
Number of special educational needs children present…

AM/PM   **POINT**

Description of each 2-minute period		5	4	3	2	1	NE
Time:	SENSITIVITY STIMULATION AUTONOMY						
Time:	SENSITIVITY STIMULATION AUTONOMY						
Time:	SENSITIVITY STIMULATION AUTONOMY						
Time:	SENSITIVITY STIMULATION AUTONOMY						
Time:	SENSITIVITY STIMULATION AUTONOMY						

Figure 3.2 Adult Engagement Observation Sheet and Interpretation Schedule (from the EEL programme, Bertram and Pascal, 1996)

development among the staff team. Practitioners are rated against a scale from 1 to 5 in each of the three areas outlined above. It may also highlight issues of wellbeing for the individual practitioner through its outcomes. If sensitivity is rated lower than might be expected, for example, this could be an opportunity for discussion as to why this is the case.

The impact of practitioner wellbeing on children's wellbeing

Research has systematically shown that the quality of children's early interactions has potential outcomes for the quality of future relationships (Sylva *et al.*, 2010). It follows that those practitioners for whom wellbeing is not an issue are more likely to respond to initiatives, and to the policies of the workplace that drive the ethos of the setting, and to a style of leadership that respects those who work at the setting in terms of what they can bring to the overall quality of provision. A feeling of positive wellbeing

Plate 2 'Successful [settings] encourage co-ordination by creating collaborative environments which encourage involvement, professional development, mutual support and assistance in problem solving'
Source: Hopkins *et al.* (1996), cited in Harris (2002: 177)

will impact on the children in their care. Rushton and Larkin (2001, cited in Zambo, 2008) argue that the brains of young children do not learn from fancy toys or information that is too rigid or too abstract; however, they do learn from everyday face-to-face interaction with adults who talk to them, who hold them and who nurture them in a loving and natural way. A healthy, happy practitioner will in turn mean a healthy, happy child.

Walsh and Gardner (2005) looked at indicators of high and low levels of motivation among adults and the ensuing impact on children in their care and the learning environment. It is worth revisiting these indicators as a useful starting point for analysis in relation to staff wellbeing. The indicators have been adapted and expanded with the birth to three years age range specifically in mind and are set out below.

According to Walsh and Gardner (2005), high levels of motivation towards their work are in evidence when the early years practitioner:

- offers stimulating, relevant and age-appropriate activities;
- shows a high degree of interest and interacts appropriately, allowing the child/children freedom, choice and opportunities to be curious, explore and investigate;
- is cheerful and enthusiastic when interacting with children and is able to maximise learning opportunities.

When high levels of motivation in relation to the practitioner's work are evident, the children are:

- happy to be left in the setting;
- pleased to see their key worker every day;
- eager to participate in what the setting has to offer;
- energetic and enthusiastic, displaying a degree of curiosity and interest in their environment.

When high levels of motivation in relation to the practitioner's work are evident, there is a subsequent impact on the environment. It:

- is spacious, airy and aesthetically pleasing;
- has a plethora of attractive and age-appropriate resources;
- is one that extends to both indoor and outdoor provision.

According to Walsh and Gardner (2005), low levels of motivation towards their work are in evidence when the early years practitioner:

- shows little interest in the children or their activities;
- directs them, dominating their activity;
- undertakes necessary care routines out of a sense of duty;
- initiates activities that are uninteresting, not age-appropriate or relevant to young children;
- offers little variety or choice;
- would prefer to interact with peers, chatting rather than paying attention to the children in their care.

When low levels of motivation in relation to the practitioner's work are evident, the children:

- appear unhappy;
- are unusually quiet or miserable;
- are apathetic and unenthusiastic;
- seem to complete an activity out of obligation rather than interest.

When low levels of motivation in relation to the practitioner's work are evident, there is a subsequent impact on the environment:

- it is dull and lacking in character;
- resources tend to be routine and uninspiring;
- children have little opportunity to use the environment available.

Looking through Walsh and Gardner's indicators of motivation, it is clear that the Adult Engagement Scale (Bertram and Pascal, 1996), in addition to highlighting the way adults interact with children and how they support their care and learning, could also be used as an indicator of wellbeing among individual members of staff in the early years setting.

Chapter conclusion

An exploration of the importance of individual practitioner wellbeing has outlined the impact for the setting as a workplace in relation to the care environment, practitioner–practitioner relationships and practitioner–child relationships. The role of the setting leader, consideration of leadership style and policy in relation to wellbeing have been considered. Maintaining personal wellbeing has also been raised and, to this end, the importance of individual self-awareness. Ways of investigating staff wellbeing within the workplace have been looked at via the use of the Adult Engagement Scale, an observation tool developed by Bertram and Pascal (1996) as part of the EEL project.

 ## Resources for further exploration

Siraj, I. and Hallett, E. (2014) *Effective Caring and Leadership in the Early Years*. London: Sage.

Siraj-Blatchford, I. and Manni, L. (2011) *Effective Leadership in the Early Years Sector. The ELEYS Study*. London: Institute of Education.

Pre-School Learning Alliance (2018) *Minds Matter: The Impact of Working in the Early Years Sector on Practitioners' Mental Health and Wellbeing*. London: Pre-School Learning Alliance. This is the relatively recent survey referred to in this chapter that brings practitioner wellbeing into the foreground of our thinking.

A Cambridgeshire charity which supports the mental wellbeing of pupils from the earliest possible opportunity can be found here: www. bluesmile.org.uk/

Support with personal wellbeing: mind.org.uk

Wellbeing within the early years setting
Supporting babies and children under three

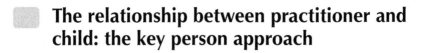

The relationship between practitioner and child: the key person approach

A theme of this early years series has been the perceived advantage of adopting a key person approach within the setting, an approach in which one person, as far as is possible, assumes overall care and responsibility for a key child or small group of key children. The case for the key person approach is outlined in more detail in Chapter 2, with activities to work through; however, you can find another related activity below. The rationale behind the key person approach is that children under three thrive on consistency; they are supported best through consistency of routine and by familiar places and patterns, both at home and in their early years setting. Consistency within the early years setting suggests an environment that is regular, predictable and constant, and it is this definition of consistency that should arguably extend to include regularity, predictability and constancy of relationships. Outcomes for the setting of a key person approach will include improved care and learning for the children, and parents and families who are confident about leaving their children there, thus supporting a child's wellbeing at an individual level whereby care is pinpointed and personalised.

Activity

The key person has a powerful impact on the wellbeing of their key children and their ability to develop and learn.

1. Where can you find allusions and references to the notion of a child's wellbeing within a key person approach?
2. How would a key person approach specifically support children's wellbeing?
3. Focusing on one of the children in your care, write down the ways in which you as their key person support their individual wellbeing.
4. Look back within previous chapters to link appropriate theory to your findings.
5. Compare your notes with a colleague's. What can you learn from each other's notes? What are the similarities? Are there any differences?

Considerations for a child's wellbeing

Wellbeing and communication: listening, understanding and responding to children from birth

The way practitioners communicate with babies and young children is a very important part of their role. Listening to children, for example, becomes an integral part of understanding what they are feeling because it is only through listening that the early years practitioner understands what it is that children need from their early years experience and is then able to respond accordingly. Degotardi and Davis (2008) explored the nature of early childhood practitioners' interpretations of young children and how practitioner responses guided curriculum decision-making processes in terms of provision. Twenty-four practitioners were asked to describe a chosen child and to interpret video extracts of that child's behaviour in the context of play and a nappy-change routine. Findings showed that practitioners differed in the degree to which they elaborated on the behaviour observed in the video extracts. To this end, Degotardi and Davis described a range of practitioner responses from 'low-elaborate' to 'highly elaborate' (p. 227). Low-elaborate responses were 'relatively short … broad, non-specific statements' consisting of 'a list of readily discernible behaviours, feelings and likes'. Such responses conveyed a descriptive rather than an interpretive approach to understanding the child's behaviour: 'She was so funny with the toy, that teddy bear' (p. 228). Degotardi and Davis' next category, 'moderately elaborate responses', included details of specific physical behaviours and a range of psychological attributes, some explanatory statements and descriptions of progressions from one behaviour to the next, making links between the child's and the practitioner's actions: 'He is quite sick this day so he's not as responsive as he normally is. He wants to do it himself without my help – he can't quite do it by himself but still doesn't want my help so I leave him to do it by himself' (p. 228).

Degotardi and Davis' final category, 'highly elaborate responses', was characterised by a clear and consistent understanding on the part of the practitioner of the links between successive behaviours and 'a sense of social and cognitive connectiveness between the infant and his/her social and physical context' (2008: 228). These responses provide a rich and varied source of interpretive statements. A final extract from their paper describes an example of a highly elaborate response:

> When we were playing the peek-a-boo box at first I don't think she really understood what it was all about, and she just stood back like, 'Whatever, OK it's a bear. I can see that.' And then she wanted to get more involved in it and help push it down [to] see sort of what happens again. And then she sort of got distracted by some of the other toys around on the floor, particularly the stacking rings ….
>
> (p. 228)

Activity

Degotardi and Davis' (2008) study is highly illuminating in that it illustrates how early years practitioners understand the children they work with. It perhaps highlights the need for ongoing professional development. The findings may encourage those reading this book to reflect on the ways in which they interpret children in their day-to-day practice.

For self-reflection

Look back through some of your recent observations for one of the children in your care. Can you place what you have written within one of Degotardi and Davis' three interpretive categories? What next steps could you take to develop your practice based on the outcome of this exercise?

Babies are sensitive to every move and gesture made by the people around them (Broomby and Bingham, 2008: 220); they are deeply interested in the people and the world in which they find themselves and they learn from what they see and experience. Not only should care and attention be paid to provision within the environment, but practitioners must be exemplary in the way they react and interact with the children in their care, and also with each other. Within the setting, children under three should see models of good, healthy adult interactions and a staff team who work together as a staff team. They should be happy to be left in the environment every day, knowing that they will be safe and cared for. If the atmosphere in the early years setting is difficult, for whatever reason, this will have an impact on children's wellbeing.

The early years practitioner needs also to be aware of the messages they are sending out to a child via their use of non-verbal language. Non-verbal language such as facial expression, effective eye contact, posture, gesture and interpersonal distance or space is usually interpreted by others as a reliable reflection of how we are feeling (Nowicki and Duke, 2000). Mehrabian (1971) devised a series of experiments dealing with the communication of feelings and attitudes, such as like–dislike. The experiments were designed to compare the influence of verbal and non-verbal cues in face-to-face interactions, leading Mehrabian to conclude that there are three elements in any face-to-face communication: visual clues, tone of voice and actual words. Through Mehrabian's experiments it was found that 55% of the emotional meaning of a message is expressed through visual clues, 38% through tone of voice and only 7% from actual words. For communication to be effective and meaningful, these three parts of the message must support each other in meaning: for example, ambiguity occurs when the words spoken are inconsistent with the tone of voice or body language of the speaker. Earlier in this book, an example was given whereby the practitioner talked to a colleague while changing a baby's nappy; not only was the baby missing out on precious one-to-one time with their key person, but consider the non-verbal messages being sent to that child.

It is important to remember that whenever we are around others, we are communicating non-verbally, whether we want to or not, and young children need to feel comfortable in the presence of the adults around them. Conversely, babies and children under three use non-verbal communication to give messages about how they feel. Babies, for example, might wave their arms or kick their legs, stiffen their bodies, arch their back or stretch and clench their fingers. Babies also move their gaze away when they are bored. Both child and practitioner should have the opportunity to work together to achieve mutual understanding through non-verbal and verbal communication, which is essential for the child's emotional development and wellbeing.

Finally, babies are surprisingly observant. The potential for supporting wellbeing through adult interaction is great. Research has highlighted young children's abilities to imitate the facial expressions, gestures and actions of others (Parker-Rees, 2007). Meltzoff and Moore (1977, cited in Parker-Rees, 2007), for example, discovered the ability of newborn babies to imitate facial expressions, most notably tongue protrusion. Babies can also recognise when their own movements are being imitated and, in choosing

Plate 3 The way practitioners communicate with babies and young children is a very important part of their role

to do just what the infant does, adults hold up a 'social mirror' (Rochat, 2004, cited in Parker-Rees, 2007) to the children with whom they interact. Because infants enjoy the companionship and familiarity associated with seeing their own behaviour returned to them with interest, they reward attentive adults with smiles and laughter, shaping the adults' behaviour; conversely, when adults find a form of interaction that works, they will therefore be more likely to repeat it. Do not tire of playing with a baby in this way! It involves precious one-to-one time and will be highly enjoyable for the baby; watch legs and arms kicking in delight and wonderful attempts to communicate via early sounds and babbles. Babies will feel cared for, liked and valued.

Wellbeing and communication: a practical suggestion

Context: From birth to about the age of 20 months, the early years practitioner can expect language development and communication skills to develop in the following ways:

- attempting to communicate in a variety of ways including crying, gurgling, babbling and squealing;
- making and experimenting with sounds with their voices in social interaction;
- taking pleasure in making and listening to a variety of sounds;
- developing a personal bank of words, or vocabulary, as they begin to develop spoken language.

Using story to develop language through interaction

Baby Touch Noisy Book (Justine Smith and Fiona Land (2007), London: Ladybird). This is a colourful first play board book with interactive features. Each page is entitled 'Baby touch', 'Baby say' or 'Baby listen'. Babies are invited to touch and investigate different textures such as the fur on the 'furry caterpillar'. A button can be pressed throughout on each 'Baby listen' page to hear a musical version of 'I'm a Little Teapot'. The text invites interaction through the interactive nature of the book, which allows babies to use most of their senses to explore, and engenders discussion with the top end of the age range outlined above that links in with some of the children's first experiences of living and learning.

Sharing the book

1. Make sure that you are familiar with the contents of the book before you share it with babies and toddlers; in this way you can find out what may be appropriate to concentrate on with them. You are aiming to encourage verbal responses from each page – sounds or words, depending on the age of the child.

2. Press the 'noisy' button and listen to the rhyme. Press the button again and sing the rhyme. You can do this as many times as the baby or young child is interested. Some might try to sing along with you, or dance as they listen to the music. As a word of warning, the book invites six opportunities to use the button and sing along noisily to the tune!

3. When you open the book to share it with a child, be guided by the text. Use the words on the page as pointers to investigate opportunities for potential responses from the children. For example, the first page suggests they 'touch the furry caterpillar'. Place a baby's hand on it and use a stroking motion while saying 'ah'. Use appropriate vocabulary to describe how the fur feels such as 'soft' and 'silky'. Note how the child responds; look for non-verbal clues such as facial expression (smiles perhaps, or eye contact with the page), as well as listening for noises such as gurgles of pleasure. Can older children repeat any of the vocabulary you use?

4. Say the simple rhyme on the first page, 'The peas in the pod go pop, pop, pop', and clap your hands once for every 'pop', encouraging children to join in.

5. Sing the octopus' noisy song on the second page. You can do this on every subsequent noisy song on the 'Baby listen' pages.

6. Use visual aids alongside the text such as a train on a track that you can model moving along as you read the fourth page together.

Older children will be able to move the train for themselves. Say 'clackety clack, clackety clack' as they do so.

7. The seventh page is entitled 'Baby say'. The idea is that the child learns to hear and then to make appropriate sounds associated with each of the four animals: the clippety-clop of the horse's hooves on the ground, the moo of the cow, the baa of the sheep and the woof of the dog. Use visual aids such as puppets or soft-toy versions of each animal to support the activity, giving children further opportunities to touch and investigate textures and talk about how those textures feel.

8. Model any suggested actions throughout, such as waving to the baby (p. 2), clapping hands (p. 5), waving to the butterfly (p. 8) and whispering (p. 9).

9. When children do repeat noises such as the animal sounds that you make, say 'That's right! The cow goes moo!' to reinforce and support language development and to encourage further interaction. Do the same when the child attempts real words and approximations of words.

Some questions to ask as you share the text

Can you press the button?

What can you hear?

Would you like to touch the furry caterpillar/sparkly helicopter, etc.?

What does it feel like?

Can you wave to the baby? (p. 2)

Where are the giraffes? (p. 3)

What noise does the horse/cow/sheep/dog make?

Can you sing the song with me?

Notes for consideration

Even books for very young children tap into their early experiences and can be a useful starting point to support the development of communication skills. Sharing books also provides opportunities for the early years practitioner to listen, understand and respond to children, as well as children having opportunities to listen, understand and respond to the practitioner. Note children's responses as you share stories with them; even at this early age they will be developing favourites that they will wish to return to time and time again. Share books as part of daily practice and routine. Find somewhere comfortable where both you and the child/children can relax and enjoy a variety of books.

Activity

Observe a colleague sharing a book with a child between the age of one and two years old. Reflect on how a child's wellbeing can be supported through sharing a story in this way.

Wellbeing, rest and sleep

Young children need sleep because it enables growth and consolidation, and is a restorative process that also allows muscles, bones and skin to grow, injuries to heal, recovery from illness and the development of a strong immune system to fight off sickness. Sleep rests the brain, but at the same time it activates it, allowing growth and enabling babies to remember what they learn, to develop increasing concentration skills, to solve problems and develop their thinking skills. We all know what it can be like trying to manage a child who has not slept. It is no fun for the adult, or for the child. Babies need to sleep peacefully, so the area within the setting chosen for sleep needs to provide peace and quiet as far as is possible. The Early Years Foundation Stage (EYFS, DfE, 2017: 30) states that 'except in childminding settings, there should be a separate baby room for children under the age of two'. A sleep area should be cosy in response to:

- recognising the child's need for a familiar sleep space by providing personal items for comfort and security;
- accommodating individual sleep patterns and habits;

- allowing early and late sleepers to be placed appropriately;
- being kept at a temperature of between 16 and 20°C (neither too hot nor too cold);
- including the planning of a quiet activity for early risers.

The early years practitioner needs to be attuned to the rhythms of the children they work with so that regular times for rest and sleep are planned within the overall period of care. Questions the practitioner might need to ask include:

- Have I asked the child's parents when their child usually sleeps at home? Am I trying to follow this routine?
- When I settle a child to sleep, am I providing consistent and sensitive care to them?
- Do I know how each child likes to be settled to sleep? If not, how can I find out this information?
- Do I understand when the children in my care show signs of being tired, needing a rest or some quiet time? How do I respond?

Activity

For self-reflection

Work through the above list of questions in relation to each child in your care. Is there any element of practice that you should think about changing? Read the case study below as food for thought …

Case study: Charlie

Charlie came to the setting at the age of 15 months. Through general discussions with his parents, his key person discovered that they often settled Charlie at night in a rocking chair before putting him in his cot. Charlie and his parents called this his 'little rock'. His key person thought it might be a good idea if she could find a similar style of chair for the setting. Charlie took great comfort from being held by his key person in the rocking chair for a short time before a sleep in the afternoon. He understood when he was tired and would look at his key person and say, 'Little rock', a pattern established at home with his parents. At first, his key person ended the 'little rock' before he was quite ready to go back in his cot. In this instance he would not settle and would call out persistently from the cot, 'Little rock! Little rock!' His key person soon learnt to gauge when Charlie was almost asleep and ready to be placed in his cot. As she put him down, she would use a reassuring, comforting voice, saying what a lovely little rock they had had together and how she hoped he would have a lovely sleep and that she would be there when he woke up. Charlie's mother in particular found his transition into full-time care (having been at home full-time with him up until this point) a little easier to bear through such an understanding response from the key person.

Wellbeing, rest and sleep: a practical suggestion

Reading a story quietly together is an option to support those children to rest who struggle to keep going when it is obvious from their tired and fractious behaviour that what they really need is to stop! Sit comfortably to read with them on a sofa or on bean bags on the floor, and let them snuggle up to you with their favourite soft toy or blanket so that they feel safe and secure – in other words, support their feeling of wellbeing.

Wellbeing and care routines

Routines for babies and children under three are important and support a major element of the need for consistency of care incorporated within an early years setting for this age group. Key persons need to find out as much as possible from parents and carers before children join the setting so that care routines followed are familiar and comforting. Between birth and the age of three is a time of immense and constant change; time must therefore be spent with each key child's family as an ongoing concern to learn about the child's changing routines, interests and dispositions. It is important to place value on care routines and not to see them as something to hurry through so that children can be moved on to activities viewed as 'educational'. Physical care is an important element of the time shared by the practitioner with babies and children under three. Make good eye contact during care routines. Provide a running commentary on what you are doing so that the child feels you are interested in them.

Wellbeing and care routines: a practical suggestion

Gathering information about individual children can be used to inform planning and focused support as well as providing key information that leads to decisions being made about the resources and experiences provided for each child.

Develop an 'All About Me' booklet for parents to fill in details about their child's routines and preferences ahead of their arrival at the setting. The booklet can be used as information for the child's key person, as a record and as a point from which to develop an appropriate care plan. Think about what information needs to be gathered and therefore the kinds of question that need to be asked within the booklet. Here are some suggestions for areas to cover:

- What important things does the child do at home? ('I can sleep in my own bed', for example.)
- How often will the child be attending the setting? (One day in the first instance, building gradually up to three days a week?)
- What does the child like to do at the setting? (Playing with favourite friends, for example.)
- What can the child do in relation to physical development? ('I can walk confidently round the room and can climb stairs', for example.)
- What are the child's interests? ('I love books and have lots of stories at home', for example.)
- What food does the child like to eat? ('Strawberries are my favourite fruit. I am learning to use a spoon to feed myself with'.)
- What does the child like to play with at the setting? ('I like to play with the train set. I have one at home'.)

How could the examples given under each area of information be expanded to give a more holistic view of the child?

Wellbeing and health

In an ideal world all the children in our care would have happy and healthy home lives and circumstances, and be happy and healthy in themselves, but sadly this is not always the case. Basic needs for any child include water, food, shelter, clothing and health care (Renck Jalongo *et al.*, 2004: 145). Sylva *et al.* (2010) reveal evidence to show that high-quality provision in the early years supports better future outcomes for children with less fortunate backgrounds. The new EYFS in England (statutory from September 2012) aims to identify children with less fortunate backgrounds by the age of two and provide additional targeted support. All children, however, are entitled to a level of protection and support in their early years environment. It is important to remember that by default all babies and children under three have special needs: the need for attention and support, for someone to feed them, to dress them and to play with them.

Wellbeing and health: a practical suggestion

Developing an interest in tasting and eating healthy food using story as a stimulus

Oliver's Fruit Salad (Vivian French (1998), London: Hodder Children's Books). Summary: fruit at home is not quite the same for Oliver after having spent time with his Grandpa, who grows everything himself in his garden. A trip to the supermarket enthuses him once more before he reveals that he did not eat any of Grandpa's fruit because he did not like it! Oliver's opinion finally changes when his grandparents visit and persuade him to try home-made fruit salad.

This book could be read with a child or a small group of children at snack time, for example, before the children share fruit together. The children could be encouraged to try some new fruits that appear in the book, such as the pineapple that Oliver has never seen in his Grandpa's garden. Have as many of the fruits described in the story as you can to support the storytelling. Put them in a role-play shopping trolley if you have one at your setting, or in a shopping basket. Create a role-play fruit and vegetable shop (perfect for two- and three-year-olds) for mobile children to access and explore. Model making healthy choices as you 'shop' with the children. Talk about why you are making such choices with the children. What would they choose?!

Another 'healthy eating' book: *Handa's Surprise* (Eileen Browne (1995), London: Walker Books).

Wellbeing and play

It was Friedrich Froebel who argued that play is part of children's nature and that children are happy when playing and learning. Play fosters emotional wellbeing and should therefore be viewed as a fundamental source of enjoyment. Early years practitioners can encourage self-expression through play, building on children's interests and supporting even the youngest of babies to play. Mobiles and singing rhymes, for example, will capture babies' interest and support their innate desire to understand and experience their world. The right to play is incorporated with Article 31 of the UN Convention on the Rights of the Child.

Wellbeing and play: a practical suggestion

Using songs, rhymes and rhythm in play

Practitioners can communicate with babies by using song and rhymes and playing musical games. Growing evidence suggests that musical activities support early language development and emotional wellbeing. Babies gain confidence as their recognition of songs, rhymes and rhythm grows. They will listen to the music from a mobile over and over again. Singing to a baby often calms them. As they grow, smaller instruments such as shakers that they can grab and hold support their understanding of cause and effect, as well as developing hand–eye coordination and fine motor skills.

Make sure that your setting is equipped with a range of age-related equipment such as musical mobiles, CDs and players (child-friendly as well as conventional) and musical instruments. A good compilation of nursery rhymes, songs and games is *This Little Puffin* by Elizabeth Matterson (1991, London: Puffin Books).

Wellbeing and inclusion

In the early years setting, inclusion refers to children, families and staff all feeling that they are accepted and valued. Practitioners must work towards

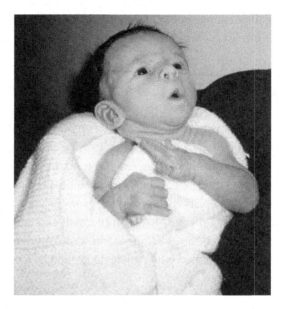

Plate 4 Play is an inherent part of children's nature

respectful relationships that value all children and their families. Inclusion also means access to an appropriate environment and resources to support every child's developmental and learning needs.

Wellbeing and inclusion: a practical suggestion

Valuing and welcoming every child in the setting

Create a photographic display of all the children and practitioners in the setting. Depending upon how your setting is organised, this could either be in the entrance hall or in each individual room. Mount each photograph so that it has a 'frame' and add the names of the children underneath. You might also like to add something that each individual child likes to do, such as playing with a particular resource; or add a statement based on observation such as 'Florence likes to play outside'. Do remember to update your babies, especially as they will change so much in a very short space of time! The display is a celebration of all the children in the setting, including their interests and achievements.

The UN Convention on the Rights of the Child

In returning to the five umbrella headings of the UN Convention on the Rights of the Child, it is possible to link elements of children's wellbeing to each of the areas outlined.

The right to a childhood

It has been argued that childhood is not a natural phenomenon, but a creation of society. However, today we take it for granted that a period of time exists in a person's life that is labelled 'childhood'. Cunningham (2006) shows how, over time, British children's roles have changed and slowly evolved along with the notion of childhood. In the Middle Ages children were not viewed as members of society, but remained on the periphery; by the time of the Industrial Revolution they had become an integral part of the workforce. In spite of the importance of the income that children brought to their families, the philanthropists of the 19th and early 20th centuries, such as Titus Salt from Bradford, West Yorkshire, viewed child labour as dangerous and a negative situation for children to be involved in. Child labour was phased out in favour of education and an emphasis on good health in the form of better diets and an active outdoor lifestyle. Throughout the 20th century, 'childhood' therefore slowly became an established and recognised period within a child's life. Underlying the principle of a right to childhood was the concept that healthy, well-educated children would become useful members of society and responsible members of the workforce. In the 21st century, childhood is recognised not only as a crucial time for growth and development, but also as a time of potential vulnerability, which means that children need extra protection compared to adults. While laws might exist to prevent child abuse, to protect children and to ensure that children attend school, and that lay down the content and standards of the school curriculum and promote healthy eating, outdoor play and exercise, many children in the world are still denied the right to a childhood as laid out in the UN Convention.

The right to be educated

Babies are born with a desire to engage with the world around them. They want to explore, and they learn by doing, by experiencing. Within an early years setting they should be given every opportunity to develop and learn, to learn about and from the people they interact with, as well as about and from the activities to which they are exposed. This is early years education, the foundation years, which set the scene for further learning to take place as the child moves on in life. A principle of learning through play should be adopted within the setting, as learning through play is an appropriate means through which the under threes can engage, explore and develop their knowledge and understanding of the world.

The right to be healthy

Article 24 of the Convention states that every child has the right to health care, clean water, nutritious food and a safe environment so they can be as healthy as possible. Measures should be taken to support health within the early years setting.

Case study: healthy eating

Raising the profile of healthy eating has been a major initiative within education in England since the early 2000s with the Health Promoting Schools scheme. The latest statutory documentation was published in 2019 and is called *School Food in England* (London: DfE). It is not uncommon for settings to have a healthy eating policy outlining aims and strategies for the promotion of healthy eating. An understanding of healthy eating is important because, in order to grow into healthy adults, children need to know about the effects that a range of food and drinks can have on their bodies, and about what they can do to help ensure healthy physical growth, as recognised within the prime area of personal, social and emotional development in the EYFS (DfE, 2017). It is important for parents and practitioners to be involved and some settings will run courses to develop understanding of nutritional issues.

Plate 5 Promoting healthy eating

The promotion of healthy eating aims to support the overall premise of the importance of a balanced diet, the impact of which will improve the physical health of children and their families through developing their awareness of the effects that foods and drinks can have on their bodies. In addition, the following may be seen as outcomes:

- an increased awareness of food hygiene and safety issues;
- an increased awareness of where some of the foods we eat come from or are produced.

It is important within the setting to ensure that children have access to healthy snacks, such as fresh fruit and vegetables, and regular drinks of fresh water. Other considerations might include ensuring that the food the setting provides takes account of individual ethical or medical requirements. If the setting provides meals, they should be healthily balanced and nutritious. If parents provide meals for their children, they should be encouraged to be healthily balanced and nutritious too. Guidelines can be developed to support parents to favour healthier options. Do remember, too, the importance of practitioners within the setting modelling eating healthily with the children; talk to them about the choices you make.

Practical responses

- Incorporate regular sessions involving food, such as the one outlined previously, within planning as part of the setting's healthy eating approach.

- Use some of the outside space available to grow, harvest and taste some foods at the setting: tomatoes can be grown from grow bags, for example, and herbs and potatoes in large pots.

- Provide healthy snacks for any drop-in groups that the setting runs.

- Include a section on nutrition in the setting library (if your setting does not have a library for parents, do consider creating one).

- Promote healthy eating through access to available resources such as recipe sheets.

- Advertise good places for recreational walks at the setting, for example, on the parent noticeboard or through a newsletter.

- Teach children the importance of checking with adults before touching unknown foods or substances, for example, berries in the outdoor area.

In addition, it is important to consider some hygiene issues with food. For children who are old enough to enjoy cooking activities, for example, it is a good idea to tie long hair back. Cover open cuts or abrasions with blue plasters (explain). Ensure those children who are old enough to enjoy cooking activities wash their hands with antibacterial soap before and after the activity; children should always be expected to wash their hands after using the toilet or before handling food.

Promoting health and safety within the setting

It should be setting policy to ensure that every reasonable step be taken to prevent injury and ill health to personnel by protecting individuals from hazards at work. This also includes children and visitors to the setting. Providing and maintaining safe, healthy and secure working conditions, training and instruction, so that all staff are able to perform their various tasks safely and efficiently, is of pre-eminence. At the same time, all staff have a legal obligation to cooperate in the promotion of health and safety within the setting. Incidents that have led or could have led to damage or injury should be reported to the manager for whom it is their duty to ensure compliance with safety arrangements within the setting. The ultimate aim of the setting is to ensure a safe and healthy working environment for all staff, children and their families, ensuring that there are sufficient facilities and arrangements for their welfare in place.

The setting manager is responsible for the effective implementation of a health and safety policy and encouraging staff, through regular monitoring, to implement health and safety arrangements. It is the duty of the setting manager to do everything possible to prevent injury to individuals. The adoption of risk assessment arrangements and procedures can support such a preventative approach. Risk assessment arrangement and procedures involve:

- Providing and maintaining safe equipment and safe systems of work.
- Making arrangements to ensure the safe use, handling, storage and transport of materials, medicines, substances and other articles.
- Providing the necessary information, instruction, training and supervision to ensure all staff are aware of their responsibilities for safety.
- Induction procedures for all new staff in health and safety.
- Providing a safe place of work with safe access.
- Providing a safe and healthy working environment.
- Providing a system for rapidly identifying and remedying hazards.

See Table 4.1 as an example of a risk assessment procedure.

The right to be treated fairly

All children have the same rights no matter where they are from, what their family background may be, or whether they are disabled or not. Currently in the UK, the fifth richest country in the world, around four million children live in poverty. Being treated fairly, however, is not restricted to economic circumstance alone; a child's wellbeing is also dependent on other factors, such as quality of care. Supportive, trustful relationships must be a goal of any early years setting. The setting should be a place where children are happy to be left and where they know they will be treated fairly. In practical terms, for babies and children under three, settings should be encouraged to value diversity and differences, have a common goal of helping all children to reach their individual potential, and recognise the importance of what children need to learn (an appropriate curriculum). Offering equal opportunities

Table 4.1 Assessment of a treasure basket

Hazard	Risk	Control measures	By whom	When
Size of objects	Baby choking	Choke tester used on all new additions to the basket – items removed if can fit through. Babies using the treasure basket to be always supervised by an adult.	Anyone who adds an item to the basket. Adult who is observing the baby exploring the basket.	Every time an item is added to the basket.
Glass items	Broken glass if damaged – cut to the skin	Only use with babies aged 6–10 months. If older toddlers present, separate an area where the treasure basket can be explored safely.	Adult supervising the activity.	Every time treasure basket is used.
Damaged objects	Children choking on small parts or cutting themselves on chipped parts	All items checked before each use of the basket.	Adult who is setting up the activity.	Before the treasure basket is used.
Cross-infection	Children catching germs	All items wiped clean after use. Any food items disposed of. Material to be put through washing machine.	Adult who has carried out the activity.	Every time treasure basket has been used.
Access to items in the basket	Heavy objects thrown/ broken causing injury	Basket to be stored out of reach of children when not in use.	Room leader.	Continuously, only used with adult supervision.

Source: www.thurrock.gov.uk/children/under3/pdf/example_risk_assess_treasure_bask (accessed 8 November 2011) does not mean treating all children the same; sometimes, to treat the children in your care equally, they will have to be treated differently.

Developing an equalities policy

An equalities policy aims to promote equality of access and opportunity for all children in the setting to play, learn and be well cared for.

For self-reflection

Think honestly about your own views and attitudes and how they might affect your work in relation to the following:

- The feelings you have towards individual children in the setting.
- The words you use with individual children or within the setting in general.
- The way you interact with individual children in the setting.

Then ask the following questions:

- Do you need to make any changes to your perceptions or views?
- How are you going to do this?

For further consideration by the setting

1. What do you offer to children in terms of resources. Do they meet the needs of all children? Consider, for example, resources to reflect different cultures, such as dolls, dressing-up clothes, cooking utensils, pretend food and musical instruments.

2. What do you offer to children in terms of activities? Do activities support and encourage children's sense of identity, belonging and self-esteem/worth? Do you develop 'gender-only' activities or do you as a setting encourage all children under three, boys and girls, to take part in all of the activities and to access all the activities you provide?

3. What are your expectations of all the children in the setting?

> *Revisit your equalities policy*
>
> Do adjustments need to be made? How will you do this as a setting? Consider the need for further training – many local services may be able to help.

The right to be heard

Article 12 of the Convention, for example, states that all children have a right to be able to give their opinion when adults are making a decision that will affect them, and adults should take that opinion seriously. Translating the right to be heard to early years practice in relation to children under three involves the skill of listening. Children develop increasingly skilful language over time with which they learn to express themselves; however, until then, listening is an integral part of understanding what they are feeling and what it is they need from their early years experience. This chapter has already established that even the newborn baby can express preferences. Most adults enjoy listening to babies and love their reactions as they engage with them. A baby's smile, for example, gives a great sense of real pleasure to many parents; a gurgle, a laugh, a baby sound, hand wave or kick all have the potential for delight and celebration. Adults listen to babies all the time, for example when they are cuddling them, feeding them, changing their nappies or bathing them. This includes the responsive practitioner who knows how to judge what the children in their care are 'saying'.

Listening and responding: helping children under three to know what will happen next

A potential cause of stress for this young age group is a sense of not knowing what is going to happen next. The settled child will understand routines and boundaries and feel safe within their care environment; however, if a child is feeling unsettled, a possible cause might be that they are having difficulty understanding the structure of the day in the setting. While it is very important to talk with children from birth, careful thought is required as to how to communicate effectively, for example, combining intonation with strong non-verbal signals such as smiling and modelling an action, or using visual clues such as covering a table with a fruit-patterned plastic cloth to indicate snack time. Aural clues are also important: playing music to indicate a tidying-up period, for example. Singing with children can also be helpful: inventing songs for each activity related to daily routines such as washing hands, getting ready for lunch, going outside, coming back in again (a very easy tune to adapt would be 'On a Cold and Frosty Morning'). One of the core messages of this book has been consistency of age-related appropriate routines to support a child's sense of wellbeing.

On a Cold and Frosty Morning

This is the way we wash our hands, wash our hands, wash our hands,
This is the way we wash our hands,
On a cold and frosty morning.

An alternative version:

This is the way we tidy up, tidy up, tidy up,
This is the way we tidy up,
On a bright and sunny morning.

Or with babies and those still needing an afternoon nap:

This is the way we go to sleep, go to sleep, go to sleep,
This is the way we go to sleep,
Sleep in the afternoon.

Remember that even the newest of babies need to hear you speak to them. They will tune into your voice, your intonation and the rhythm of your utterances. A final thought in relation to this section is to ensure that you help children to pace themselves with an activity; if you are leading a singing time, for example, alert children to the fact that you are going to sing one last song together rather than singing the song and then telling your group that singing time has come to an end. You could tell them what will happen next: 'We are going to sing one last song together and then it will be time to put on our coats and go home!' Young children do benefit from signposting through language in this way. They are offered structure, reassurance and consistency through knowing what is going to happen next.

Making expectations clear for children under three

While the skill of listening to children is an art form in itself, how the practitioner uses words to communicate effectively is also important. Although aspects of communication have been covered earlier in this book, it is worth considering the use of questioning within the setting. What do you think a child's response might be to the following question, for example?

'David, shall we tidy up now?'

David could quite happily say 'No!' if asked this question. It is open-ended, clearly allowing him a choice of either yes or no. It is imperative that the early years practitioner understands the language they use with children in their care. Sometimes when a question is asked, a choice is available; in David's case, however, the practitioner is more likely to have been *telling* him to help tidy up the setting so that they could move on to another phase in the day. In her mind there was no choice; the expectation would have been that he would have happily said, 'Yes!' and done what he was being 'asked' to do. This is not what David heard or, indeed, what she communicated to him through her question. A better way of communicating to David what the next steps were would have been to say:

'David, it's time to tidy up now. What are you going to tidy away first?'

Activity

Consider the use of questioning within the setting. Do you as staff take a consistent approach? Which of the following questions allow choice and which do not?

1. Can you put your coat on your peg?
2. How many bricks can you put away in the box?

3. How do you put your wellies on?

4. Would you like apple or banana?

5. Shall we change your nappy now?

6. How are you today?

7. What did you have for breakfast today?

8. Do you need to go to the toilet?

9. Do you need a drink?

10. Let's go outside, shall we?

How might you rephrase some of the above questions to make your intentions clearer and so support children's understanding in terms of what they hear?

Chapter conclusion

This chapter has focused on the relationship between good early years practice and children's wellbeing. The concept of the key person is outlined to show how this approach allows for regularity and predictability for children under three, important foundational elements of their wellbeing; the benefits are briefly explored. Communication is a recurring theme that is explored throughout the chapter under various umbrellas of thinking, in particular in relation to listening and responding to children under three and choosing clear language structures that enable understanding on the child's part. The role of non-verbal communication is considered alongside the aural aspect. Issues of inclusion and health and safety are also explored. Practical suggestions link together theory and principles of care with good practice.

Resources for further exploration

Pascal, C., Bertram, T. and Rouse, L. (2020) *Getting it Right in the Early Years. A Review of the Evidence.* St Albans: The British Association for Early Childhood Education.

For support materials outlining a strong, succinct overview of aspects of child development from birth, look at pages 48–58 in Siraj, I., Kingston, D. and Melhuish, E. (2015) *Sustained Shared Thinking and Emotional Well-being (SSTEW) Scale for 2–5-year-olds Provision*. London: Trentham IOE Press.

The United Nations Convention on the Rights of the Child website can be found here: www.unicef.org.uk/what-we-do/un-convention-child-rights/

5

Wellbeing
Principles into practice

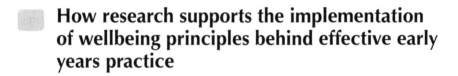

How research supports the implementation of wellbeing principles behind effective early years practice

Several studies have shown that good quality early years education can have a positive effect on the educational, cognitive, behavioural and social outcomes of children, in both the short and long term (Sylva *et al.*, 2010; Taggart *et al.*, 2015). This book has made a clear link between the quality of early years education and care given to babies and children under three and their positive wellbeing, which in turn impacts readiness to learn and develop. It is therefore important to consider how research might further inform and reinforce effective early years practice for this age group. One of the most recent studies undertaken in England has been the Study of Early Education and Development, or SEED (Melhuish and Gardiner, 2020). SEED is a longitudinal study, with the aim of evaluating:

- the effect of early education on children's outcomes;
- the quality of early years provision;
- value for money of providing government-funded early years education.

Background to the study

Since September 2010, all three- and four-year-olds in England have been entitled to funded early education for 570 hours per year (commonly taken as

15 hours per week for 38 weeks of the year). More recently, the government expanded this entitlement to benefit two-year-old children living in the most disadvantaged households in England. From September 2013, two-year-old children living in households that were within the 20% most disadvantaged by household income became eligible for 15 hours of funded early education per week. This was extended in September 2014 to two-year-old children living in households within the 40% most disadvantaged by household income. SEED was designed to help the Department for Education provide evidence on the effectiveness of early years education and to identify any short- and longer-term benefits from this investment.

Conducted in waves, SEED was designed to follow a cohort of children from the age of two years each year until the age of five, and then finally at seven years old, evaluating their outcomes vis-à-vis the Early Years Foundation Stage Profile (EYFSP), the current document for recording children's progress in the early years in England, on a yearly basis. Data from the first three waves of the survey is available from the UK Data Service:

- SEED wave 1 data (two-year-olds);
- SEED wave 2 data (three-year-olds);
- SEED wave 3 data (four-year-olds).

While there is not the space here to go into every detail of the study, a link between the quality of aspects of a child's home learning environment and their wellbeing has emerged (Melhuish and Gardiner, 2020: 26).

Home learning environment

A higher home learning environment was associated with better outcomes on all EYFSP measures during reception and better verbal ability during school year one.

Household disorder

Higher levels of household disorder were associated with poorer outcomes on all EYFSP measures during reception and with poorer outcomes on all socio-emotional measures, with the exception of externalising behaviour.

Parent psychological distress

Higher parental psychological distress was associated with lower child sociability.

Limit setting

Higher levels of limit setting were associated with better outcomes on all EYFSP measures, with the exceptions of personal, social and emotional development and numeracy, and with better verbal and non-verbal ability. In contrast, higher levels of limit setting were also associated with higher externalising behaviour and with lower emotional self-regulation. In interpreting these negative associations, it is possible that poorer socio-emotional outcomes may be a consequence of higher limit setting, but also higher limit setting may be a response to children's challenging behaviour.

Warmth in the parent–child relationship

Higher levels of warmth in the parent–child relationship were associated with better outcomes on all EYFSP measures and with better verbal ability. Higher levels of warmth were also associated with better outcomes on all socio-emotional measures.

Invasiveness in the parent–child relationship

Higher levels of invasiveness in the parent–child relationship were associated with poorer outcomes for EYFSP communication and language.

Authoritarian parenting

Higher levels of authoritarian parenting were associated with lower verbal ability during school year one.

Permissive parenting

Higher levels of permissive parenting were associated with poorer outcomes for EYFSP literacy and numeracy, EYFSP good level of development and EYFSP total score.

While offering a mere snapshot of part of the overall findings here, the key point to make is that the theory which has been explored within this book shows how the outcomes are strongly linked in relation to the above, particularly Bowlby's Attachment Theory in Chapter 2.

Activity

Revisit Chapter 2 at this point to refresh your memory in relation to Bowlby's Attachment Theory, and reflect on Melhuish and Gardiner's (2020) findings. What might the implications be for your setting? Write down some notes and use them for the remainder of this chapter, as well as its suggested actions for reviewing setting provision in relation to supporting children's wellbeing.

Supporting wellbeing: developing a high-quality early years setting

Issues to consider when reviewing setting provision in relation to supporting wellbeing include the following:

1. Revisit the setting mission statement.

    Suggested action: What elements of wellbeing can you currently include within the statement? Does the mission statement need to be revised in any way to include a more overt acknowledgement of the importance of supporting a child's wellbeing?

2. Consider the needs of parents and the partnership that you cultivate with them.

    Suggested action: In the light of the content of this book, consider the following questions:

- Why is it important to share information with parents?

- Why is it important to respect parents' preferences concerning the care routines for their children?

- How do parent–setting relationships impact on the notion of well-being within the setting?

3. Consider whether the setting provides appropriate environments for the children (book 1 in this series, *Appropriate Environments for Children under Three*, looks extensively at reviewing provision in this way to provide the optimum experiences for this age group). Suffice it to say that babies and children under three derive security from an environment that is regular, predictable and constant, thus supporting the foundations of their wellbeing. To support individual wellbeing, the available space must be thought about carefully: active play areas should be clearly separated from quiet areas, for example. As much as possible, the defined areas should be permanent for this age group, allowing them to learn through familiarity and repetition. Dempsey and Frost (1993) argue that arranging the space in this way will help children to focus on available materials or resources in that area and will also encourage play and interactions with peers.

   Suggested action: Review the setting environment. In relation to each area, ask the following:

   - Is each area being used to the optimum?

   - Is children's wellbeing supported within every area of the setting, and throughout the early years curriculum in place? How do you know? (i.e. What evidence do you have?) Look at the example below of supporting wellbeing through creativity as a starting point.

4. Setting staff must work as a team to determine achievable and age-appropriate rules and to set clear boundaries based on realistic expectations of baby and toddler behaviour. Children learn through repeated explanation and by experiencing and responding to the rules and structure of the setting. These are best reinforced by the establishment of a regular, ordered environment. Children should be invited to help maintain this order, and to understand it. Putting away toys is a major part of the setting day, for example, and it is a good idea to try to slow down the process to give enough time for children to become involved.

Suggested action: Think carefully about the following key points, both individually and then as a staff team:

- Do you consider yourself to be a team player?
- What changes could be made to ensure effective communication takes place throughout the setting?
- How will any changes be implemented?

Supporting wellbeing through creativity within the early years setting

Consider whether as a staff member you value the creative processes children go through as they approach activities and learn and develop within the setting environment. Practice that includes providing pictures for children to colour in, or producing identical cards with the same picture on front where the practitioner has obviously intervened, for example to ensure the picture looks 'conventional', involves little creativity. Here are some points to reflect on in relation to current practice:

- Allow children to develop hand–eye coordination and fine motor skills through activities that ensure that they are the genuine authors of their creations; value their expressive outcomes and do not alter what they have produced to fit an adult's idea of what is 'right'.
- Whenever possible, be flexible and work at the pace of the child; allow children plenty of time to explore and express their ideas; if a child becomes engrossed in carefully building a structure with bricks, let them do so. Take photographs of the process for parents who confuse the notion of outcome (a final product) with success.
- Ensure children have regular access to a full range of experiences within the setting. Support their interests through the resources you provide.
- Consider self-expression. Do children have the opportunity to represent their ideas in different ways?
- Do those that work at the setting encourage parents to value the creative processes children go through?

Key point

Focus on the process in any creative activity, not the end product. Make sure your activities focus on what the child is getting from the activity. What are they experiencing? How is it supporting their learning and development?

 ## Supporting wellbeing: wellbeing and experiences

How well does the setting support the following areas for development?

Developing three-dimensional awareness and representation

From birth to one year, children:

- experience the world in three dimensions;
- handle, feel and manipulate three-dimensional objects and materials using their senses, including using their hands, fingers and mouth;
- use their eyes to explore form;
- enjoy manipulating food;
- experience three-dimensional construction such as mobiles.

From one to two years, children:

- heap objects and demolish structures;
- mix and stir flour and water (and other similar substances);
- manipulate dough and clay;
- tear and crunch paper and card.

From two to three years, children:

- construct ready-made forms such as blocks, bricks and boxes;
- use construction materials, such as blocks, horizontally: for example, they will line up bricks to create (represent) a road;
- stack, roll and line up objects;
- use their hands to roll, pinch and coil dough and clay.

Developing musical awareness and skills

From birth to one year, children:

- are sensitive to dynamics and timbre: for example, they are startled by loud sounds;
- respond to the human voice and recognise the sound of their mother's voice;
- read emotion in voices;
- are comforted by lullabies and engage in vocal play;
- associate sound with things.

From one to two years, children:

- imitate adult vocalisations and the melody and rhythm that appear in them;
- engage in musical performance;
- are interested in the source of sounds and manipulate materials to produce sound, for example, tin lids;
- use both hands when making sounds.

From two to three years, children:

- attempt to imitate sound or tune and use melody patterns from learnt songs spontaneously;
- explore the sound potential of household objects;
- can use hands independently and clap to rhythm in song.

Key point

Ensure your knowledge of how children learn and develop from birth is secure. How does your knowledge impact on your approach to provision for the children in your care? Do you resource activities according to this knowledge?

Supporting wellbeing through understanding the newborn baby: seeing the world in black and white

While a newborn baby can see from birth, their vision is not as clear as that of an older child or adult. Until the age of six months, a baby will respond best to bold, contrasting colours. Objects with patterns having 100% contrast, such as black on white, are the easiest for a young baby to see. Providing a baby with black-and-white contrasts will captivate and hold their attention, encouraging visual development as well as physical activity such as kicking, waving arms and wriggling. Think about creating a black-and-white area within the setting, or a treasure basket of black and white resources. Include material with black-and-white patterns such as tea towels, plain black material to place white objects on, plain white material to place black objects on, a collection of both black and white objects, and a mobile of black-and-white contrasting patterns. What else could you include?

Key point

Remember that babies prefer the human face to any other object or pattern; they are programmed to search out and stare at human faces because it is from people they will learn the most. It is imperative to keep your face close, smile, talk and make eye contact with babies.

Activity

Use Figure 5.1 to develop a pro forma to use within your setting with a view to supporting individual wellbeing through targeted provision.

Could it be adapted in any way to suit your setting? Does the pro forma work? How might it support future practice in relation to supporting individual children's wellbeing?

Name	Erin
Age	19 months
Context	Free exploration in the role-play area
We observed . . .	Erin likes to play in the role-play area; it is a favourite area of the setting for her. She keeps opening and shutting the doors to see what's inside and finding resources from other areas of the room to put in the washing machine.
We thought . . .	We could add some resources that might encourage Erin's interest in filling and emptying and her notion of 'What's inside?'
We tried . . .	Adding large pasta shapes, real fruit and vegetables, scarves and some bags.
We found out . . .	1. Erin was fascinated by the addition of bags and began to place resources carefully inside them, picking up one object at a time. 2. She played for extended periods of time. She also transported the bags all around the room, showing the contents to practitioners.
We changed . . .	We decided to leave these resources out for a few weeks and observe Erin's play before changing anything.
Next we will . . .	Consider what other areas of the learning environment could be used to support Erin's interest in filling and emptying.

Figure 5.1 An example of how wellbeing can be supported through responding to a child's interests

Chapter conclusion

Chapter 5 has highlighted some of the issues to consider when taking a reflective review of setting provision in relation to supporting children's wellbeing. It has taken into account findings from a significant recent study in England with a view to providing a strong rationale for change, where change is needed, within an early years setting, in order to develop effective practice.

 # Resources for further exploration

Melhuish, E. and Gardiner, J. (2020) *Study of Early Education and Development (SEED). Impact Study on Early Education Use and Child Outcomes up to Age Five Years: Research Report.* London: DfE.

The Department for Education website, which contains all the SEED study reports, can be found here:

www.gov.uk/government/collections/study-of-early-education-and-development-seed

6 Drawing the threads together

The true measure of a nation's standing is how well it attends to its children – their health and safety, their material security, their education and socialisation, and their sense of being loved, valued, and included in the families and societies into which they are born.

(UNICEF, 2007: 1)

Early childhood education and care

The recognition of early childhood education and care (ECEC) embraces the first stage of lifelong learning. More than ever before, organisations such as UNESCO, UNICEF and the World Bank are prioritising ECEC in their policies and programmes. Much attention is being paid to increasing access to young children to ECEC services, to ensuring and measuring quality of ECEC programmes and to assessing young children's learning outcomes. The notion of ECEC is therefore relevant here, because it incorporates both the concept of education and that of appropriate care: two elements that are inextricably linked for this age group. While a key role for early years practitioners is to support the children they are responsible for in being able to gradually understand the world around them, babies and children under three need practical support with personal care until they can eventually begin to start to share in their own care of dressing, feeding and toileting. In this respect, self-help skills can be thought of as developing akin to the Vygotskian principle of scaffolding, as discussed in Chapter 2.

On a practical level, instilling basic knowledge in very young children. such as the names of everyday objects and colours and number and letter recognition, might also arguably equip them with the tools they need to get an educational head-start; however, children need to learn how to learn and to make sense of their environment through effective communication. As discussed earlier in this book, knowing how to listen and respond to babies and children under three is a key role of the effective early years practitioner. The importance of ECEC in babies and children under three extends further to include their early development skills and how they are supported to become – eventually – adults who have the tools to function well socially, economically and culturally within their society. Children's development is supported when they feel part of the routines that mean each day runs smoothly; very young children experience a personal satisfaction in being a helper to adults. Saying 'Thank you' and smiling when a child passes you their cup will encourage them to repeat this action on subsequent occasions, as well as acknowledging them as individuals who (a) have the ability to contribute and (b) whose contribution is valued within the context of the setting. Feeling valued in this way supports individual wellbeing. Ordinary routines support learning and development, such as when children are tidying up; they learn about simple time management, and putting objects back where they belong, respect for the environment through keeping it tidy, and how to work alongside others cooperatively.

It is important to consider the term ECEC because our changing society means that more and more children are spending time in early years settings while their parents work. This is why it is so important for the early years practitioner to understand the dual nature of their work with this age group. The fact that the early years practitioner is working with and alongside parents in undertaking the care element of children under three is perhaps one of the most helpful ways of perceiving the value of their specialist role. International research evidence shows that a child-oriented conception of ECEC may lead to better outcomes, especially with regard to children's socio-emotional development, interests and (learning) motivation. These factors are again crucial for children's later school success and children's ability to become active members of society.

Case study: Norway's new kindergarten education framework

Early childhood education and care (ECEC) programmes can offer a wide array of benefits to children, parents and society at large – provided they are of high quality. Since the 1999 OECD Thematic Review of ECEC in Norway, the country has undertaken major policy reforms to expand access to, and improve the quality of, the country's kindergartens. The Norwegian Agency for Quality Assurance in Education, or NOKUT (www.nokut.no/en/), undertook an evaluation of the kindergarten teacher education system in 2010, after which a new framework for kindergarten teacher education was developed. This new framework is closely linked to the now statutory Norwegian Framework Plan for Kindergartens (2017), which takes into account children's well-being, their development and learning, and which stresses the value of childhood, children's voices and a child-oriented approach to learning and development. The changes to kindergarten teacher education, originally implemented in 2013, emphasise the value of the kindergarten as an institution providing education and care for the whole period of early childhood before the beginning of primary schooling. The title of the profession was changed from pre-school teacher to kindergarten teacher to emphasise the value of kindergarten in its own right, rather than just as preparation for school. Norway's approach thus points to the holistic understanding of education, giving wellbeing and socio-emotional development a special place in ECEC.

Wellbeing and quality provision within the early years setting

Wustenberg and Schneider (2008, cited in Wertfein et al., 2009: 20) argue that there are seven important quality indicators for the daily care of babies and children under three. Looked at in relation to the planning process in book 2 of this series, *Planning and Observation of Children under Three*, it is useful to revisit them here in relation to a child's wellbeing:

1. The individual adjustment process. This is about how every child is supported to settle in within the setting. It is important to remember that while a setting might have a broad overarching policy to introduce families and their children to the care environment, Wustenberg and Schneider (2008, cited in Wertfein *et al.*, 2009) emphasise the *individual* in their concept of the adjustment process. This is therefore a process that should be reviewed on an ongoing basis in relation to every individual child because there will be periods, for example after illness or holidays, that have the potential to unsettle an otherwise settled child. It is this attention to detail in relation to the individual that will support their personal and emotional wellbeing within the setting.

2. A familiar person (or key person) who the child accepts and responds to. The key person provides continuity of care for an individual child and acts as a key link between home and the setting, ensuring that close communication with parents is maintained. This relationship enables the kind of information that will help provide continuity of care between the home and the setting to be overt and available. It is also the kind of information that will ensure that a child's wellbeing is of paramount importance when addressing their individual needs.

3. Warm and stable relationships between practitioner and child. All children like to be liked (Parker-Rees, 2007) and it goes without saying that all children respond to love, kindness and understanding. For those children who might have a more impoverished home life in this respect, the setting, through providing high-quality care, plays a key role (Sylva *et al.*, 2010).

4. Orientation towards a child's needs, interests and wellbeing. (See in particular point 2 above.) Oberhuemer (2005) argues that there is now a general consensus that early childhood curricula should meet the child's needs and interests, in turn supporting healthy wellbeing.

5. Nurturing relationships, healthy nutrition and a clear, daily routine. All of these encompass a strong emphasis on personal wellbeing.

6. Materials and activities that stimulate the child's exploratory drive. It is important to resource the setting appropriately, or at least to review provision to ensure that current resources are being used to the optimum effect to satisfy the curiosity and inquisitive nature of babies and children under three. Appropriate resources support a child's wellbeing through

offering them the opportunities to develop and feel good about themselves in what they achieve: making a shaker shake, for example, or taking their first few steps with a trolley.

7.   A local network of resources and specialists for both children and their parents. Parents of babies and children under three often need support; in addition, they have a right to expect high-quality, flexible services that respond to the changing needs of their families. Not only does a key person play a significant role in supporting parents, but settings must consider their range of provision extending to the particular needs of the community they serve. These might include, for example, classes they offer, or specialist talks they arrange; important notices displayed clearly where parents will see them; and contact numbers for local organisations and services. Offering relevant services will impact on the wellbeing of the wider community, families and their children attending the setting.

Final thoughts

Child wellbeing in 'rich' countries: some of the facts

UNICEF's *Report Card 7* (2007: 2) provides a comprehensive assessment of the lives and wellbeing of children and young people in 21 nations of the industrialised world. Measurements are taken against six dimensions: material wellbeing; health and safety; educational wellbeing; family and peer relationships; behaviours and risks; and subjective wellbeing. Some of the main findings are as follows:

- The Netherlands heads the table of overall child wellbeing, ranking in the top ten for all six dimensions.

- European countries dominate the top half of the overall league table, with Northern European countries claiming the top four places.

- All 21 countries have weaknesses that need to be addressed.

- The United Kingdom and the United States of America find themselves in the bottom third of the rankings for five of the six dimensions reviewed.

- There is no obvious relationship between levels of child wellbeing and GDP per capita. The Czech Republic, for example, achieves a higher overall rank for child wellbeing than several much wealthier countries, including the United States and the United Kingdom.

A main aim of the UNICEF research into child wellbeing is to discover whether children 'feel loved, cherished, special and supported within the family and the community, and whether the family and community are being supported in this task by public policy and resources' (2007: 39). It is this sentiment that has pervaded the issue of how best to support the wellbeing of babies and children under three throughout this book. Wellbeing, as discussed in Chapter 1, is notoriously difficult to define, and therefore a definition was reached that looked specifically at wellbeing within the early years setting for babies and children under three; one that focuses on providing an appropriate environment in which children are cared for according to individual need. Childhood, according to the UN Convention on the Rights of the Child, is a crucial time for growth and development, and getting the foundational input right for babies and children under three has been another focus for scrutiny within these pages. It is clear that there is no room for complacency, and this is echoed in countries such as England in revisiting early years curricula to decide how best to develop a curriculum that reflects the need for appropriate early input. Changing work patterns dictate a need for high-quality early years environments where parents feel happy to leave their very young children, where those children are happy to be left, and where they can thrive supported by dedicated early years practitioners who understand and respond to their needs.

> They [early years practitioners] are specialists who understand and respond to babies' and young children's needs, both physical and emotional; specialists who can support developing social skills, who interact willingly with the children in their care and who share conversations fuelled by mutual enjoyment of genuinely shared interests. Specialist practitioners know how to develop the early years environment to support young children's individual needs.
>
> (Bradford, 2012: 8)

In this way, wellbeing is incorporated within early years curricula, alongside effective pedagogy and practice. It is part of the early years setting ethos and is embedded holistically across individual need.

 # Postscript

Wellbeing and 21st-century phenomena

The world is currently in the grip of a global pandemic that has threatened the very fabric of everyday life and society. Every country in the world has been affected. Schooling has been put on hold in the majority of countries, and this has included early years provision. As babies and children under three gradually return to their early years settings, practitioners will need to support their wellbeing as these very young children experience yet another significant change in their young lives, having become accustomed to being at home again. Consider the implications for attachment as a once familiar routine at the setting feels unfamiliar once more; consider the worried parent whose anxiety the child might pick up on, but not fully understand, meaning that drop-off times become stressful for both. How will your setting support the families and children so that a sense of 'normality' can return? And your own wellbeing and that of those who work in the setting? What next? The Early Intervention Foundation in the UK offers a range of advice and support based on fact and is currently embarking on a two-year project which aims to support the development of children's skills and capabilities by strengthening the quality of early childhood education in the UK; this will be in the light of current evidence. Children's books have been published to help explain the pandemic to young children. Include a strand within your wellbeing policy that takes into account the impact of these changes on our lives, and on those of the children in our care. This is not something new; as early years practitioners, we can continue to offer good practice, whatever the circumstances around us, and be guided by the best research in creating the best possible response and approach.

References

Ainsworth, M.D.S. and Wittig, B.A. (1969) Attachment and exploratory behaviour of 1-year olds in a strange situation, in B.M. Foss (ed.) *Determinants of Infant Behaviour (Vol. 4)*. London: Methuen.

Alexander, R. (2010) *Children, Their World, Their Education*. London: Routledge.

Bertram, T. and Pascal, C. (1996) *Effective Early Learning: An Action Plan for Change*. London: Esmée Fairbairn Charitable Trust.

Bowlby, J. (1969) *Attachment and Loss (Vol. 1)*. New York: Basic Books.

Bradford, H. (2012) *Appropriate Environments for Children under Three*. London: Routledge.

Braungart-Rieker, J., Garwood, M.M., Powers, B.P. and Wang, X. (2001) Parental sensitivity, infant affect, and affect regulation: predictors of later attachment. *Child Development*, 72 (1): 252–270.

Broomby, H. and Bingham, S. (2008) 'We are passing the smile around.' Personal, social and health education in early years, in D. Whitebread and P. Coltman (eds) *Teaching and Learning in the Early Years*, 3rd edn. Abingdon: Routledge.

Cunningham, H. (2006) *The Invention of Childhood*. London: BBC Books.

David, T. (2009) Young children's social and emotional development, in T. Maynard and N. Thomas (eds) *An Introduction to Early Childhood Studies*, 2nd edn. London: Sage.

David, T., Goouch, K., Powell, S. and Abbott, L. (2003) *Birth to Three Matters: A Review of the Literature Compiled to Inform the Framework to Support Children in their Earliest Years. Research Report 444*. London: DfES Publications.

Degotardi, S. and Davis, B. (2008) Understanding infants: characteristics of early childhood practitioners' interpretations of infants and their behaviours. *Early Years*, 28 (3): 221–234.

Dempsey, J.D. and Frost, J.L. (1993) *Play Environments in Early Childhood. Handbook of Research on the Education of Young Children*. New York: Macmillan.

Department for Education (2013) *Early Education and Childcare: Statutory Guidance for Local Authorities*. London: DfE.

Department for Education (2017) *Statutory Framework for the Early Years Foundation Stage*. London: DfE.

Elfer, P. and Dearnley, K. (2007) Nurseries and emotional well-being: evaluating an emotionally containing model of professional development. *Early Years*, 27 (3): 267–279.

Ereaut, G. and Whiting, R. (2008) *What Do We Mean By 'Wellbeing'? And Why Might It Matter? Research Report DCSF RW073*. London: DCSF.

Florez, I.R. (2011) Developing young children's self-regulation through everyday experiences. *Young Children*, July 2011: 46–51.

Galinsky, E. (2010) *Mind in the Making: The Seven Essential Life Skills Every Child Needs*. New York: HarperCollins.

Goleman, D. (1996) *Emotional Intelligence: Why It Can Matter More Than IQ*. London: Bloomsbury.

Harris, A. (2002) *School Improvement: What's In It For Schools?* London: Routledge.

Laevers, F. (1994) *The Leuven Involvement Scale for Young Children*. Manual and Video. Experiential Education Series, No. 1. Leuven, Belgium: Research Centre for Experiential Education, Leuven University.

Laevers, F. (1996) Social competence, self-organisation and exploratory drive and creativity: definition and assessment. Paper presented at the 6th European Early Childhood Education Research Association Conference on the Quality of Childhood Education, September 1996, Lisbon.

Laevers, F. (2005) (ed.) *Well-being and Involvement in Care Settings. A Process-oriented Self-evaluation Instrument*. Leuven, Belgium: Research Centre for Experiential Education, Leuven University.

Main, M. and Solomon, J. (1990) Procedures for identifying infants as disorganized/disoriented during the Ainsworth Strange Situation, in M.T. Greenberg, D. Cicchetti and E.M. Cummings (eds) *The John D. and Catherine T. MacArthur Foundation Series on Mental Health and*

Development. Attachment in the Preschool Years: Theory, Research, and Intervention. Chicago: University of Chicago Press.

Malaguzzi, L. (1993) For an education based on relationships. *Young Children*, 49 (1): 9–12.

Male, T. and Nicholson, N. (2016) Leadership, in I. Palaiologou (ed.) *The Early Years Foundation Stage.* London: Sage.

Maslow, A.H. (1943) A theory of human motivation. *Psychological Review*, 50 (4): 370–396.

Mayr, T. and Ulich, M. (2009) Social-emotional well-being and resilience of children in early childhood settings – PERIK: an empirically based observation scale for practitioners. *Early Years*, 29 (1): 45–57.

Mehrabian, A. (1971) *Silent Messages.* Belmont, CA: Wadsworth.

Melhuish, E. and Gardiner, J. (2020) *Study of Early Education and Development (SEED). Impact Study on Early Education Use and Child Outcomes up to Age Five Years: Research Report.* London: DfE.

Moss, P. (2010). *What is Your Image of the Child? UNESCO Policy Brief on Early Childhood No.47.* Paris: UNESCO.

Moyles, J. (2006) *Effective Leadership and Management in the Early Years.* London: McGraw-Hill UK.

National Institute for Health and Clinical Excellence (2009) *Promoting Mental Wellbeing Through Productive and Healthy Working Conditions: Guidance for Employers.* London: NICE.

National Institute for Health and Clinical Excellence (2012) *Social and Emotional Wellbeing: Early Years.* London: NICE.

National Institute for Health and Clinical Excellence (2017) *Healthy Workplaces: Improving Employee Mental and Physical Health and Wellbeing.* London: NICE.

Nias, J., Southworth, G. and Yeomans, R. (1989) *Staff Relationships in the Primary School.* London: Cassell.

Noddings, N. (2002) *Starting at Home. Care and Social Policy.* Berkeley: University of California Press.

Nowicki, S. and Duke, M. (2000) *Helping the Child Who Doesn't Fit In.* Atlanta, GA: Peachtree.

Oberhuemer, P. (2005) Conceptualising the early childhood pedagogue: policy approaches and issues of professionalism. *European Early Childhood Education Research Journal*, 13 (1): 5–16.

Parker-Rees, R. (2007) Liking to be liked: imitation, familiarity and pedagogy in the first years of life. *Early Years*, 27 (1): 3–17.

Pascal. C., Bertram, T. and Rouse, L. (2020) *Getting it Right in the Early Years. A Review of the Evidence*. St Albans: The British Association for Early Childhood Education.

Pollard, E.L. and Lee, P.D. (2003) Child well-being: a systematic review of the literature. *Social Indicators Research*, 61: 59–78.

Pre-School Learning Alliance (2018) *Minds Matter: The Impact of Working in the Early Years Sector on Practitioners' Mental Health and Wellbeing*. London: Pre-School Learning Alliance.

Renck Jalongo, M., Fennimore, B.S., Pattnaik, J., Laverick, D.M., Brewster, J. and Mutuku, M. (2004) Blended perspectives: a global vision for high-quality early childhood education. *Early Childhood Education Journal*, 36: 87–92.

Roberts, R. (2006) *Self-Esteem and Early Learning*, 2nd edn. London: Paul Chapman.

Siraj, I., Kingston, D. and Melhuish, E. (2015) *Sustained Shared Thinking and Emotional Well-being (SSTEW) Scale for 2–5-year-olds Provision*. London: Trentham IOE Press.

Siraj-Blatchford, I. and Manni, L. (2011) *Effective Leadership in the Early Years Sector. The ELEYS Study*. London: Institute of Education.

Strehmal, P. (2016) Leadership in early childhood education – theoretical and empirical approaches. *Journal of Early Childhood Education Research*, 5 (2): 344–355.

Sylva, K., Melhuish, E., Sammons, P., Siraj-Blatchford, I. and Taggart, B. (2010) *Early Childhood Matters: Evidence from the Effective Pre-School and Primary Education Project*. Oxford: Routledge.

Taggart, B., Sylva, K., Melhuish, E., Sammons, P. and Siraj, I. (2015) *Effective Pre-school, Primary and Secondary Education Project (EPPSE 3–16+): How Pre-school Influences Children and Young People's Attainment and Developmental Outcomes Over Time. DfE Research Brief, June 2015*. London: DfE.

UNICEF (2007) *Report Card 7. Child Poverty in Perspective: An Overview of Child Well-being in Rich Countries*. Florence: UNICEF Innocenti Research Centre.

Wallach, V. and Caulfield, R. (1998) Attachment and at-risk infants: theoretical perspectives and clinical implications. *Early Childhood Educational Journal*, 26 (2): 125–129.

Walsh, G. and Gardner, J. (2005) Assessing the quality of early years learning environments. *Early Childhood Research and Practice*, 7 (1): 27–57.

Wertfein, M., Spies-Kofler, A. and Becer-Stoll, F. (2009) Quality curriculum for under-threes: the impact of structural standards. *Early Years*, 29 (1): 19–31.

World Health Organization (1948) Constitution of the World Health Organization. Drawn up by the International Health Conference on 7 April 1948, New York.

Zambo, D. (2008) Childcare workers' knowledge about the brain and developmentally appropriate practice. *Early Childhood Education Journal*, 35: 571–577.

Index

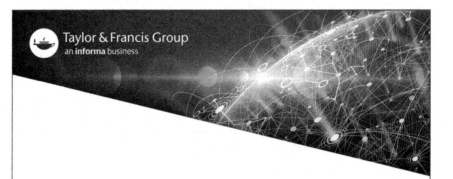